Shared
Authority
on Campus

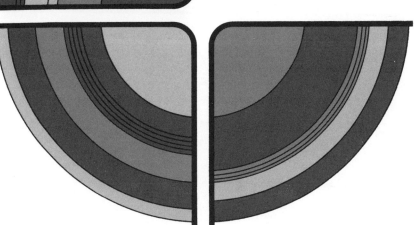

by MORRIS KEETON

in collaboration with

STEPHEN PLUMER • HAROLD HODGKINSON • GEORGE STERN
RUTH CHURCHILL • MICHAEL METTY

A REPORT ON THE CAMPUS GOVERNANCE PROGRAM
of the
AMERICAN ASSOCIATION FOR HIGHER EDUCATION
One Dupont Circle, Suite 780, Washington, D.C. 20036

Library of Congress card catalog no. 76-151810

Price: 1-9 copies $3.75 each
       10 or more copies $3.00 each

The Campus Governance Program, a project of the
American Association for Higher Education, was
made possible by a grant from the Charles F. Kettering Foundation. The Association is grateful to
the Kettering Foundation not only for its continuing
financial support of the program over the past years,
but for its tolerance and understanding during those
times when circumstances required a reassessment
of the goal and of the way to reach it. Such cooperation is invaluable in any expedition into difficult
terrain. Thanks are due also to the Esso Education
Foundation, which provided assistance in preparing
and disseminating this publication, and to the many
persons who have aided in the study. The most
active of these individuals are named in Appendix B.
The report itself is a statement of the judgments of
the director of the program and not of the sponsor-
ing organizations.

Contents

Chapter 2.

WHAT THE CAMPUS CONSTITUENCIES SEE AND SAY/38

Chapter 3.

CONSENT, ACCOUNTABILITY, AND LEADERSHIP/101

SUMMARY OF RECOMMENDATIONS/146

List of Exhibits and Tables

Introduction

A TASK GROUP ON FACULTY AUTHORITY

When the Campus Governance Program got under way in 1966, unionization of faculty and the threat of strikes were in the air. A task group led by Arnold Weber of the University of Chicago studied thirty-five colleges and universities to seek clues to the causes of faculty unrest. The task group met in a series of one- and two-day working sessions to debate proposals for reform. The key recommendation of the task group was that faculty should have a greater share of governing authority than they had on the troubled campuses at that time.[1]

In 1966 student unrest and campus disruptions had not reached the frequency or the magnitude they would shortly reach, but it was clear that fundamental discontent with campus governance and communications was by no means confined to faculty. On many campuses students also felt that they were in the dark about what was really going on. Both faculty and students felt that they did not hold the levers of genuine power. Some regents complained that the president and deans stood between them and the campus to block effective use of the legal powers of the governing board. Numerous deans felt hemmed in by the noncooperation

---

[1] Weber, 1.

1

of students and faculty, on the one hand, and by the autocracy or timidity of the president, on the other. A growing number of presidents reported themselves unable to get on with the task of the university because the trustees, faculty, students, alumni, and public were hopelessly at odds with one another. In every quarter there was a sense of impotence.

If a cure for faculty unrest lay in granting the faculty a greater share of authority, would a similar answer cure the frustrations experienced by students, administrators, and trustees? For each of these constituencies, the case for greater voice in campus affairs was appealing. But taken together these cases presented a paradox. How could each group add to its power without another group losing?

Some scholars on organization and management replied that sharing authority is not necessarily a win-or-lose "game." The widespread feeling of disfranchisement may be justified; some of the conditions, attitudes, and assumptions governing the campuses prevent effective collaboration and restrict all of the parties in what they can accomplish. If the keys of this restriction can be discovered and replaced, it may become possible for faculty, students, administrators, and trustees all to achieve more of what they seek.

The prospect of everyone's aspirations being well served is ideal, but is it realistic or wise? What if the campus interest groups are fundamentally opposed in their purposes? What if campus conflicts turn in great part upon narrow self-interest, inexperience, or incompetence on the part of one or another of the conflicting groups? What if outside forces impose restrictions which make collaboration impractical, as when a legislature requires open admissions but limits tuition charges and state appropriations? What if campus unrest is in part a symptom of a clash of political ideologies and life styles?

These questions made it clear that the difficulties of campus governance are a tangle of many threads. To unsnarl them and to reweave them is a task that combines at least four different types of work: (a) conceptual analysis to clarify what is involved; (b) fact gathering; (c) imaginative construction of alternative possibilities for governing, and (d) practical judgment as to what is feasible in specific campus contexts. In practice these tasks cannot be isolated from one another. For example, what facts should be gathered? The answer depends upon what has been shown to be important by analysis and upon what alternatives to present arrangements are seen as desirable and practical.

A CHOICE OF STRATEGY:
THE NINETEEN CAMPUS STUDY

A search of literature was undertaken in 1966–67 to guide the Campus Governance Program staff in the choice of data we should seek. We found little well-developed theory on the nature and processes of campus governance. Much writing on the subject borrowed directly from research on organization in industry, a parallel which left us with doubts. Most of the remaining work on campus governance was based upon the authors' experiences in a limited number of institutions, often in only one or two. Research instruments for gathering data had not been created to articulate with a well-developed idea of the functioning of a campus in its governance and management.

After discovering the lack of existing knowledge the staff designed a Nineteen Campus Study which was a conscious "shot in the dark." Fundamental to the design was the assumption that the prerogatives in governing and managing a campus should be more widely shared. This assumption has been reinforced by our findings and experiences in the Study, but the meaning and the implementation which we initially gave to the assumption have altered substantially during the Study. For example, an initial emphasis upon the means of sharing power has given way to emphasis upon the climate of acceptance of authority relationships. Similarly, an early stress upon participation in governing bodies as a means of enfranchisement has given way to emphasis upon the diversity of means for fostering consent and energetic pursuit of campus objectives.

Further decisions on what method would serve the inquiry best were as follows:

1. An intensive study of a few campuses with both questionnaire and interviews would further our understanding better than reliance upon a nationwide questionnaire study only. Resources dictated that the sample be not more than twenty campuses. With the aid of the Planning Committee, we selected and enlisted nineteen campuses with diversified types of control and educational programs, regional location, size of enrollments, complexity of organizations, and academic climates. The point

of this diversity was not to achieve representativeness, but to permit observation of the range of different circumstances and problems likely to affect efforts to improve campus governance.

2. We would learn more by using student, faculty, and administrator interviewers than by using only one or two of the three. Interviewers were enlisted from the institutions being studied (to serve on other campuses), the staff, and the Society for Religion in Higher Education, which is made up of Kent, Danforth, and postdoctoral Fellows. Training of these interviewers began at the "Week of Work" conducted by the Society at Oberlin College in the summer of 1967. The faculty and administrator interviewers in turn invited mature undergraduate and graduate students to work with them.

3. We would get a more accurate picture of campus conditions by asking our questions of students, faculty, administrators, and trustees than by asking only two or three of these groups. Like photographs of the same object from different angles in different light, the testimonies of different perceivers would give essential and complementary evidence on the same complex activities of governing. Every event or problem on a campus can be seen from many individual perspectives, we reasoned. There is no such thing as one individual perception of a campus event or problem that is a complete or correct view. The best possible grasp of an event or problem would be a composite which accounted as fully as possible for the disparities and congruencies of different individuals' perceptions and reports, all of which must be taken as valid data. An adequate approach to governance will reflect this conception of how to describe and understand events and problems on campus.

4. A direct survey of opinions about how to improve governance would be less productive than would a study of problems, contexts, and patterns of coping with problems through the processes of governing and managing. At the same time, the staff members prepared opinion papers and solicited such papers from others in order to be in touch with current thinking about causes and cures for campus difficulties in governance.

5. After devising several trial questionnaires, we adopted a quite simple idea about what to ask our different witnesses. In governing a campus, people confront problems and opportunities with limited resources and with purposes of varying clarity and

compatibility. In this activity, some people are more knowledgeable than others. Some are more influential than others. We would try to discover how different groups viewed the problems, the persons with influence and information, and the efforts to cope with the problems in serving the ends. Questionnaire data could yield a quantifiable overview of the campuses' problems and contexts. Interviews would give these quantified data a more specific meaning and local color and would help to see the bearings of the quantified data upon a general understanding of campus governance.

The Nineteen Campus Study has produced recommendations on two subjects: who should have prerogatives in governing and managing and on what grounds (Chapter 1), and how these prerogatives should be exercised (Chapter 3). Both sets of recommendations—who should govern, and how—are normative. No factual data can prove such recommendations. The data have a different function. They offer examples of effective and ineffective practice. They disclose the complications in both present practices and prospective ones. They provide material for analysis and speculation. The function of the data in such an inquiry is not to prove conclusions, but rather to shape them, to enable those who govern and manage to see more clearly what is involved in the various alternatives. For example, if the use of representative councils is to be recommended for a large, complex campus, what do our data show about the costs, difficulties, and conditions for practical implementation of this idea? What alternative modes of influence and control might be practical? Such questions are treated in Chapter 3.

THE CONTEXT OF CAMPUS GOVERNANCE: THE COLLEGE TRUSTEE STUDY

The most important defect of our Nineteen Campus Study in its gathering of campus perspectives was the small access it had to trustee thinking. An ideal complement was Morton Rauh's plans to do a national study of who trustees are, what they do as trustees, and how they think about their own institutions and about higher education. Rauh received responses from 5,180 trustees serving 536 institutions of higher education selected to reflect the different modes of control and levels of educational offering available. This study was independently conceived and conducted, but drew support from the Campus Governance Program, and has provided helpful data and analysis.

Our effort to understand campus governance and to suggest substantial improvements was complicated from the outset by the likelihood that some of the campus conflicts of the 1960's went deeper than disagreement about internal methods of governing. They were, perhaps, in part a response to disorders of the contemporary world. In many cases, however, the conflicts also signaled a crisis of confidence in the purposes and leadership of the colleges and universities. There was on many campuses a growing awareness of lack of consensus, distrust of leadership, dissatisfaction with the institutional roles of colleges and universities in society, and an emerging long-term change in the cultural climate and life style of many institutions of higher education.

If the governance problems of a campus are in part a challenge to the rightness of its purposes and priorities, an appeal to the law, the charter, and the bylaws does not end the difficulty. The challenge may entail a demand or a plea not merely to change that constitution, but to change the basis and methods upon which constitutionality is determined.

We have assumed throughout this study the rightness and desirability of a system of higher education in America in which different colleges and universities are governed by differently constituted boards of control using different patterns of further allocation of authority. Even within this century, however, there have been striking changes in the makeup of student bodies, in the priorities for higher education recognized by the federal and state governments, and in the social context in which colleges and universities serve. It would be a surprise indeed if, as a matter of practical conduct of campus affairs, changes of such significance did not in turn call for substantial changes in the allocation of authority and responsibility. That these changes should also reach to the level of change in the makeup of the boards of control seems predictable.

Rather than debate at length an ideal allocation of authority, either at board or at other levels, we have proposed a reconsideration of authority relationships with a view to a more effective hearing for students, faculty, and other inadequately heeded campus constituencies. We will present reports on campus contexts and problems and on the perceived sources of information and influence to illustrate the inputs to deliberation and decision making which such a change of authority relationships would permit. Finally, we will discuss recommendations on the processes of consent, accountability, and leadership which would enable those who share authority in campus governance to exercise their authority responsibly and effectively.

The Constituencies and Their Claims

THERE IS NO SIMPLE FORMULA as to who should govern an American college or university. Four grounds for claiming the right to share in governing are put forward:

1. Those whose concerns and lives are most affected by campus activities should surely have a part in their control.

2. Those who are most competent to do the work of the campus should have a voice that ensures the effective use of their competence.

3. Those whose cooperation is essential to the effectiveness of the campus in its work should have a place in governing that facilitates their continuing cooperation.

4. Those whose sponsorship and resources created and sustain the institution, and thus make possible the opportunity of higher education, are entitled to protect and further their purposes and interests.

DIFFICULTIES IN SATISFYING THE CLAIMS

These four grounds for a voice in governance can be presented both as ethical claims to rights and as practical requirements of effective campus operations. In this study, emphasis is put upon the practical requirements of effectiveness. If a "constituency" is defined as a group whose sponsorship, cooperation, competencies, or concerns are important to the work of a campus, then each campus has numerous constituencies. Once the merits of any claims to a share of authority are granted, we still do not know how these claims can be effectively implemented. The very existence of diverse grounds for authority with different applicability to different groups presents a difficulty in deciding who should govern.

A further complication in the inquiry as to who should govern is the fact that legal control and effective day-to-day control in the crucial campus choices need not be the same. To enfranchise a group who can help the institution succeed better, it is not necessary that the group sit in the board of trustees or in the university senate. How the group can thus obtain the optimum influence and power and how it can ensure continuance of an optimum relationship is a question involving both formal and informal authority and permitting the use of a great variety of means.

A third difficulty lies in the effect of changed circumstances. Changes of circumstance in turn change who is most affected, who is most competent, whose cooperation is essential, and even at times whose sponsorship and resources sustain the campus. A substantial change of circumstances can thus have a major effect in determining how an abstract right to influence can best be implemented.

In the past decade there has been unusual attention on American campuses to these complexities and to the need for realignment of authority to reflect a deliberate judgment by the parties in conflict about the issues. Where the issues have been debated and resolved, the outcome has generally been an increased provision for formal voice and vote for faculty, students, or both. The question here as to who should govern is not primarily a question about participation in boards, councils, and committees. It is a question of the influence and effect appropriate to the rights and responsibilities of those who constitute the campus and its constituencies. Assuming the four bases for influence just stated, what application do they have to the claims for governing authority by faculty, students, and other constituencies of today's campuses?

GROUNDS FOR FACULTY AUTHORITY

The primary justification for faculty voice in campus governance is the fact that faculty alone have the kinds and degree of qualification essential to the task of the college or university. They are selected and appointed on the basis of those qualifications. Most faculty are teachers; some are researchers; others are specialists in other forms of public service provided by their institutions; and many combine these competences. In the subject matter in which they teach, serve, or do research, the great majority of faculty are further specialized as philosophers, physicists, historians, economists, sociologists, biologists, or the like.

Normally the faculty as a professional body represent a further type of competence—that of experience and commitment. Though faculty mobility has in the past quarter-century reduced the average span of faculty service, the turnover of presidents has changed even more dramatically; trustees rotate more commonly than was once the case; and even those students who pursue uninterrupted studies have a short tenure. The largest element of continuity and experience with the tasks and problems of the campus is increasingly that of the faculty.

Because of their tasks and competences, the faculty's cooperation is essential if the work of the campus is to be done. Between 1965 and 1970, this point came home forcefully when faculty on a number of public campuses struck or threatened to strike. Faculty strikes at public colleges and universities are illegal in most states. Yet even that onus did not prevent strikes during this period. Moreover, the means of noncooperation available to faculty are many: educational sanctions, political sanctions, and economic sanctions. Often more destructive than a full strike are forms of the "partial strike" in which minimum legal requirements of their jobs are met by faculty while other professional activities are curtailed. The use of these sanctions, however, marks a situation that is disadvantageous for both faculty and campus.

The Campus Governance Program's Task Force on Faculty Representation and Academic Negotiations (1967) urged that the overwhelming consideration in fixing the role of faculty in governance should be the desire to improve the performance of the institution. If this is so, the necessity of faculty cooperation should be seen as a problem of how to maximize the use of faculty competences in meeting campus objectives. Involvements in governing can ensure and energize both cooperation and the devotion of faculty expertise to improvement. The full participation of their own representatives in crucial decisions can win a faculty's belief in the rightness of a policy or decision when otherwise it would not seem credible to them. Bringing their knowledge and perspective to a problem as decision about it is shaped can win their cooperation and improve the solution.

Basing the case for faculty voice upon the utility of faculty competence and the necessity of their cooperation is a counsel of prudence. Their right to a voice and vote may also be rooted in the claim of a human right to take part in the shaping of policies that affect one's life and well-being. In the case of faculty this self-determination in matters of their expertness and their work is also a crucial part of the meaning of being a professional. The concept of the professional, in turn, is a derivative of social experience as to how best to develop and muster competence to serve the ends which men choose. The prudential and ethical grounds for a faculty share of campus authority thus double back on one another: the ends a campus may practically pursue depend upon the power of the means available, and the power of these means depends upon the opportunity of faculty to share in the choice of the ends.

There are those who argue that the campus is not to be confused with society, and that the sponsors of a college may appropriately alter the rights of those who opt freely to work for and with particular sponsors, be they public or private. The point is well taken. But if the purposes of the sponsors include a concern for both a free society and the role of reason within it, their own purposes imply that they must hear and heed the faculty.

In some institutions the faculty themselves are the sponsors or a significant part of the sponsorship of a college. Where faculty are represented as sponsors, their rights in governance should reflect it.

There are difficulties and disadvantages to faculty participation in campus governance. A party at interest in a decision affecting others may press his interest improperly at their expense. In a complex matter, an expert is prone to overestimate the weight of that part of it in which he is expert. Moreover, in rendering a service an expert may not rightly arrogate to himself the client's rights in choosing the type and priorities of service he intends to obtain. Those who have most experience with a task fall too easily into the assumption that new circumstances do not alter the way it can best be done. Those with greatest continuity in an organization become too readily pre-occupied with institutional maintenance at the cost of changes of purpose or work which might better serve the trust for which the institution exists. The use of faculty time to govern with-draws that time and talent from the tasks for which the faculty were employed and in which they are most expert.

How do the bases for faculty sharing in campus authority and the disadvantages of their doing so permit a resolution of the question as to their proper role in governance? That resolu-tion can take form through specific attention to the relevance of faculty competences, cooperation, and interests in the specific types of policy and decisions being shared. For example, it is obvious that physicists must help with the design of a univer-sity's electron accelerator. So should pedagogues help with the design of teaching spaces. The staffing of a clinic would not be determined without substantial use of expert medical knowledge and experience; the same applies to the staffing of instruction. At the same time, the physicists may not be given carte blanche to spend at will (the public purse must be protected, and economy may force the scientists to invent other means to their ends), and staffing must be managed within the bounds of cost and purpose set by others than the professional doctors or teachers.

If influence is to follow the contribution which each con-stituency of an institution can best make, the mechanisms and channels for influence will have to reflect this complexity and interweaving of essential contributions and essential precautions against constituency biases and limitations. The Task Force on Faculty Representation worked out in some detail the bearing of this principle upon the different roles appropriate to faculty on issues such as educational and administrative policy, personnel administration, economic arrangements, and public policy.[1]

Current practice leaves a great deal to be desired if faculty are to be accorded influence fitting to the principle just stated. In 1966-67 the Task Force studied thirty-five campuses where the issues of faculty voice were in ferment. The Task Force judged that the sample underrepresented campuses where faculty had acquiesced to administrator dominance and possibly also underrepresented those with faculty dominance, faculty primacy, or shared authority. The Task Force estimated that about 50 per-

---

[1] Weber, 1.

cent of the campuses studied were marked by administrative primacy, another 25 percent by shared authority between faculty and administration, only a few campuses by faculty primacy, and most of the last 25 percent by administrative dominance.[2]

If qualification to contribute and disabilities in doing so were to govern the definition of constituency roles in governance, the concepts of dominance and primacy would be appropriate only with respect to particular types of policy and decision. For example, interviewers in the Nineteen Campus Study, which followed that of the Task Force, felt that teaching assistants and younger faculty (often unrecognized even in faculty senates) were inadequately represented in the consideration of personnel and economic issues directly affecting their interests. If rank and experience bear any positive relationship to disciplinary competence, competence in pedagogy and research, or contribution through continuity, it is appropriate that older faculty win the bulk of senate leadership and other such roles. At the same time, the older faculty's interests may conflict directly with those of younger faculty on issues of pay and working conditions, and the perspectives of younger faculty, closer in age and often in life style to their students, may require representation in policy deliberations if pedagogy is to be best served.

The Task Force also found a defect of representation in systems which place crucial authority over higher education in coordinating boards, superboards, or state administrative offices and legislatures. In these situations faculty often were provided no vehicle or poor vehicles for their own representation at the levels of governance where decisions were actually made. Again the decision as to the level of taxation to support public higher education is appropriately reserved to publicly chosen representatives or their delegates. It is not prudent or right, however, to screen these public representatives from knowledge or interaction with those who can best present the interests, relevant knowledge, and experience of faculty to them.

A similar problem of representation in denominational colleges may call for a different resolution. In one such college an impasse between trustees and faculty, with administration in the middle seeking to mediate, was resolved by establishing regular participation of faculty and students in trustee committees and occasional, more inclusive, informal meetings of trustees

---

[2] *Ibid.*, pp. 16-17.

with faculty and students. In Catholic institutions where faculty have often been dominant numerically in the controlling board, they have often failed to exercise an independent perspective because they were members of the controlling church order and were appointed by the college president or the presiding bishop.

A final example of types of inadequate faculty role in governance emerged in the course of data taking in the Nineteen Campus Study. The data do not dictate, but suggest, that faculty in different disciplinary groupings (e.g., humanities or social sciences as contrasted with applied sciences or administrative studies) bring different perspectives and priorities to campus concerns (see Highlight 3 in Chapter 2). On a few issues the age of faculty correlated significantly with their reporting of problems and their reflection of priorities in interviews (see Highlight 7 in Chapter 2). Interviews showed that in recent campus unrest about ethnic studies and ideological issues it was helpful to problem solving if faculty representative of the contending factions could be formally involved in efforts to work out resolution of the issues. Some of the groupings significant for governance were persistent and could appropriately be reflected in the formal structure of governance; others were transitory and might best be treated through ad hoc legislative or administrative mechanisms.

WHAT VOICE FOR STUDENTS—AND WHY?

Teaching is primarily for students. They are the principal learners. They are the original clients for the campus services. On private college campuses they or their families are also consumers in a second sense: they pay most of the cost. On public campuses they pay an increasing share. It is their daily lives that are most affected by policies on campus life and the conditions of learning. How should the interests of client, buyer, and resident be protected and represented in campus governance?

In higher education, some say, the buyer must beware. He has many choices of campuses. Once he has chosen, he should not complain; or, to be more precise, he is entitled to only such relief as complaint will gain. He is a petitioner, without further rights. Moreover, he is a petitioner whose preferences may not serve his own best interests. Others know best, or at least better than he.

But, without his help, do they know best? And is his choice of campus altogether free? Granted that his interests as learner and resident may be his paramount basis for a say in campus affairs, is learning an enterprise in which his cooperation and his competences play a crucial part if the campus is to achieve its greatest effectiveness?

Higher education in the United States is more accessible than ever before, but it is far from unrestricted for those who qualify, and far from being open on equally manageable terms to all. The Carnegie Commission on Higher Education, in its recommendations for improving access, has stressed particularly the present inequities deriving from low income, ethnic origin, geographic location, age, and prior schooling.[3]

The high demand for access to college and graduate school combined with limited room in the most preferred institutions has compounded the sense of restricted opportunity. The pressure to go to college for reasons of economic and social advancement has for some decades removed higher education from the sphere of "entirely optional goods" for many people. During the period of peacetime draft with mandatory college deferments, this sense of coercion was heightened. The student thus often faces a forced choice with half-open options. In buying toothpaste the consumer enjoys some protection by way of the governmental regulatory agencies; but in higher education the service to the individual cannot be subjected to laboratory tests that apply to a product dispensed nationwide. In most cases only the student in the classroom gets a reliable sample. The damage cannot be repaired by refund or recall of the service. Some better method of learner representation must be found.

Although the interest of a student as client may seem to be his paramount basis for a right to vote and voice in campus governance, it is probably a poorer basis for discerning his optimal role than is the contribution he can make to the effectiveness of the campus. In higher education the cooperation of the learner is absolutely essential to good results. He can give or withhold that cooperation in multitudinous ways and on many different dimensions of his work as learner. The damage he can do to campus effectiveness is a far less helpful basis for designing his participation in governance than is the promise he alone can

---

[3] *A Chance To Learn.* New York: McGraw-Hill Book Co., March 1970.

make real, but both the potential damage and the realizable promise are substantial.

The Task Force on Faculty Representation pointed out in 1967 that the damage from outright strikes of faculty may well be less than that of less visible forms of withholding cooperation. While demonstrations, cessations of classes, and physical damage dramatize potential damage, they do not always cut at the heart of the work of a college or university as deeply as does a failure to commit oneself to inquiry, to do more than go through the motions of learning, or to accord respect for dissent and reasoned investigation. Sometimes both violence and the repudiation of intellectual searching go together. Sometimes campus violence is, albeit misconceived, an expedient of protest against an already prevalent neglect or repression of genuine inquiry. Needed in the design of the students' roles in governance are ways to combat both the internal and external threats to the very essence of the intellectual function—inquiry—and at the same time to activate the initiative and competence of students in pursuing that function.

Aside from petition and persuasion, the main resort of students for influence on campus in the past has been noncooperation and selective cooperation. The elective system was a mode of enfranchisement of students. Their choices of majors and elective and "service" courses play a heavy role in the allocation of faculty positions, departmental support, and eventually facilities and degree programs. As options on housing and dining services have been opened in recent years, students' selections have slowed down dormitory building programs and have bankrupted some options in dining services. In some colleges today there is more than one way for a student to meet each or some of the degree requirements, with the result that courses which become unfavorably known on the campus grapevine may have to be dropped or altered. "Voting with the feet" is a crude instrument for deliberation and reform in an enterprise as sophisticated as a college or a university. Nevertheless, it has sometimes been more effective than committees in eliciting change.

If the effort to prevent damage should give way to that of furthering learning, what competences of students are available to a campus? These vary tremendously from a community college located to serve primarily a low-income population of students with poor educational backgrounds to a leading research university whose graduate students are already among the brightest

and best educated of citizens. Nor is the advantage all with one
or the other of these disparate student populations. One student
group may have a realism about social conditions, a knowledge of
political maneuvering, a sensitivity to prejudices, a clarity of
purpose, and an acceptance of self that the other shares less fully.
The other may have a great edge in knowledge, verbal facility,
understanding of the dynamics of society, and mastery of the
processes of technical inquiry. Both may offer an important
complement and perspective to faculty and administrator views
about the gaps between announced objectives of curricula or
courses, on the one hand, and their actualities, on the other hand:
the utility to students of requirements about the sequence and
packaging of courses; the relevance of studies to the life and
vocational aims of the students; the selection of faculty who work
and communicate effectively with students; the recognition of
good or poor faculty performance in instruction and counseling;
and the creation of student "peer cultures" or campus climate
which enhances achievement of institutional goals. The advantages which students bring to these tasks are in part those of
opportunity to observe and experience, in part those of perspective, and in part those of acting as a counterforce to special
interests of faculty or administrators which are not always in the
best interests of the institution.[4]

For the practical demands of campus governance, one of the
most useful ways to view potential student contributions to governance is to examine the requirements which campus purposes
place upon campus life and instruction under contemporary conditions. For example, students arrive on campus today more
mature than did those of a century or a half-century ago, and the
college is expected to contribute further to their maturity. In
contemporary society matters which once were considered appropriate for institutional regulation are now defined as properly
matters of personal choice as long as there is not interference
with other people. While the definition of what is private and
personal varies among American and collegiate subcultures, there
has been change throughout American higher education on the
proper scope and nature of parietal regulations. Even the sharpest critics of some forms of student role in governance normally

---

[4] For both bibliography and a statement of the pros and cons of students'
sharing the power to govern, see Earl J. McGrath. *Should Students Share
the Power?* Philadelphia: Temple University Press, 1970.

grant the importance of their taking part in the creation and application of these regulations. Given a society in which change and mobility make even the ordinary citizen's life less protected and stable than before, the task of developing maturity in students cannot be well done if they themselves do not take major responsibility for the quality of student life. To insist otherwise is demeaning of their maturity and futile in practice. Moreover, it builds resentment and resistance against legitimate exercise of authority in other quarters.

Still more critical is the relation between learning and self-determination. A scholar is a person who wants to learn, chooses his own objectives in learning, and knows how to enlist competent assistance in choosing the ends and means of further inquiries. An inquirer who is not a mature scholar should be on the way toward the capacity for scholarship. Some college instruction is still a matter of acquiring information on how to do a job or how to pass a certification test, and some students are present primarily to escape adult responsibilities or to get a degree. But these practices, where they exist, are deficiencies to be overcome, a caricature of what higher education should be. If the capacity for self-determination in learning and in life is to mature as it should in students, the conduct of life and instruction on campus must elicit growing autonomy among them. No particular structures of governance are implied by that requirement, but a climate acceptant of students' sharing in critical decisions and mechanisms suited to the particular campus will be increasingly essential to effectiveness.

The difficulties and disadvantages of student participation in governance are substantial, and in practice these must be heeded if both student and institutional interests are to be well served. Students are charged with transiency, inexperience, immaturity, ignorance of crucial aspects of campus governance, special interests that conflict with institutional goals (e.g., keeping charges at a minimum), and lack of sufficient time and interest to do well with the responsibilities of governance. The principle proposed for designing a faculty role in governance should apply to students as well: Design the role to obtain the contributions available from student competences and cooperation and to protect the other constituencies and the institution against undue effects of the special interests and limitations that apply on the particular campus.

The failure of "free universities" to persist and thrive follows from failure to apply this principle. What they gained in
relevance to student concerns was lost in discontinuity and
shortage of faculty and administrative competence. When established institutions are studied in the light of the principle, there
has been a remarkable change in practice since the early 1960's;
but participation in campus governance is still much less effectively provided for students than for faculty. Earl McGrath
reports that in the fall of 1969, 88.3 percent of 875 institutions
replying had admitted some students to membership in at least
one policy-making body. When the specific boards, councils, and
committees with student membership are studied and the specific
roles of students are noted, the process can be seen as a significant
but incomplete step toward the recommended collaboration. For
example, in more than half of McGrath's reporting institutions
students had achieved membership on curriculum committees.
In 22.7 percent students were on executive committees. Twenty
percent of the institutions had admitted students to board meetings, but they had voting privileges in only 2.7 percent. Only
41 of the 875 institutions had admitted students to committees on
faculty selection, promotion, and tenure; and in only 12 of these
could students vote.[5]

In designing the structures and processes by which students
exert power in campus governance, some further considerations
should also be kept in mind. Among these are the relative effectiveness of informal processes where the intention to share
authority is genuine and pervasive, the need for different patterns
of participation on different types of policy and program decision,
and the possibility that an adversary proceeding may be the only
effective means available or the best of the feasible options when
an impasse develops. The Task Force on Faculty Participation
spelled out these possibilities with respect to faculty participation
in governance under different circumstances. In Chapter 3 these
factors also play a part in the recommendations about consent
and accountability as applied to student constituencies.

It is also important to keep in mind that students differ
among themselves even more than do faculty or campus administrators. Extensive research is already available about the
variety of American student cultures. A single university campus
sometimes harbors several distinctive subcultures. Neither stu-

---

[5] *Ibid.*, pp. 38-50 and Appendix for further details.

dents nor faculty may be thought of as a single constituency, a monolith of opinions, values, and interests. For example, in Chapter 2 we report the fact that on some issues third-year students identify more clearly with disciplinary groups (such as humanities and social sciences faculty) than with other students. On some ideological issues, the groupings are less appropriately identified as student groups than as radical or conservative constituencies which cut across faculty, student, and other lines. Similarly, certain ethnic minorities which see themselves as having a particular cultural mission enlist and organize across faculty, student, and noncampus groupings. To cope with this pluralism of identities of individuals and groups and with their changing character, campus governing structures and processes will need a flexibility and complexity uncommon in our presently complex society.

THE PROPER POWERS OF ADMINISTRATORS

In most colleges and universities, as reported already, the administrators are dominant. The Task Force on Faculty Representation considered the administrators too powerful in the great majority of campuses, and almost never underrepresented. The sharing of authority with other constituencies clearly involves curtailment of that power.

To curtail administrative power at a time when there is a public outcry against campus disorders may seem the reverse of what is needed. Three distinctions may be helpful in seeing why the sharing of some powers may actually strengthen the hand of administrators in their proper roles. First, the sharing of legislative authority is not to be confused with a sharing of managerial powers, though legislative policy does set the purposes and policies within which management operates. Second, the management tasks in a college or university are partially carried out by faculty and students, as in the faculty's management of instruction and the students' assumption of some tasks of dormitory management or control of social life. A division of labor on these tasks may facilitate the performance of administrative functions rather than hinder it. Third, the surrender or sharing of particular powers in policy making or management can strengthen the administrative leaders in other functions and in their capacity to achieve the overall goals of the institution. For example, under certain circumstances the use of honor systems has been more effective in limiting cheating than instructor proctoring; administrative efforts to exert direct control over academic standards is generally less effective than insistence that faculty carry responsibility for those standards; and the delegation of budgetary control over lines within departmental budgets is often more effective in both fiscal and educational outcomes than detailed preauditing of all expenditures by the central administration.

Prior to World War II college presidents typically achieved outstanding results by their powers of charisma, competence, and prerogative. As campuses became large and complex, these resources ceased to suffice, particularly for institutions striving to become excellent in their field. Under contemporary circumstances, administrators must find ways to exercise their leadership which draw upon the capabilities and the willing cooperation of the leaders of the other campus constituencies.

The dominant claim of administrators to voice and vote in the policy making of a campus is that of their essential competences. At the levels of leadership, they are chosen for these competences. They may be removed from office if they fail in either competence, support of constituencies, or cooperation with the board and the other administrative leaders. The tasks of administrators put them in a unique position to have or to obtain the information crucial to understanding and solving the institution's problems and to achieving its purposes. As professionals, they have an interest in working conditions which maximize their capacity to do their tasks well. Crucial among these conditions is that of being free to carry out their work in a manner of their own choosing and to know at the outset the limits within which this choice is theirs.

Because of the intimate relationship between policy and implementation and the importance of good information to wise policy making, direct participation of major administrators in policy-making bodies is a normal part of currently recognized good practice. Thus presidents sit ex officio on boards of trustees, and deans take part ex officio in the councils shaping policy for the deans' jurisdictions. The presence of the administrators is more critical than whether they have vote as well as voice. Often campus committees are served regularly by administrative staff who do not vote but who supply essential data and judgments on the effects of alternative policies. A formal vote for administrators is a way of making sure that everyone on a board or in a council is aware of the administrators' judgment. Since the administrators' convictions bear heavily upon their ability and willingness to make the councils' and committees' actions work, the formal vote also helps to ensure a workable agreement.

OTHER CAMPUS CONSTITUENCIES

Other groups claim, or have had made in their behalf claims to, a share of authority in campus governance: alumni, parents of students, staff other than faculty and principal administrators, and constituencies peculiar to a particular campus or type of campus. Most of these are, or can best be, represented in boards of trustees or in advisory boards for the particular programs in which they have an interest.

The most neglected constituency is the nonfaculty staff. In confrontations that closed campuses, these staff have often been the ones whose economic interests suffered most. Unionization is a resort for them where it is not prohibited by law, but it is not as direct a route to influence upon noneconomic issues as would be representation in the committees and councils which deal with employee interests. Moreover, the active cooperation of these staff, like that of students and faculty, is essential to full effectiveness, and many of them bring competence and perspectives to campus policy problems that would complement the resources otherwise available.

TRUSTEES: THEIR MAKEUP AND CHANGING ROLES

A college or university is a public trust. In the American polity, even a private college bears this character. The legal basis for trustee authority is a charter issued by a state or, in rare cases, by the federal government. All of the seventeenth-century American colleges were private, though in the small and close-knit communities of that time the private–public distinction hardly had the meaning which it has today. The rise of public colleges and universities, particularly since the Civil War, and the sharply increasing proportion of public campus enrollments since World War I have introduced a division of labor between private and public institutions which is still undergoing change. A growing self-consciousness about institutional purposes has resulted from these trends and from efforts to divide labor efficiently and apply limited resources effectively to the improvement of performance.

In his work on trusteeship, Morton Rauh identifies the principal tasks of trustees as three: choosing the mission or purposes of the institution, choosing and replacing the chief executive at appropriate times, and making sure that the management of the institution is good. In state systems of higher education, the trustees or regents may be subject to, or dependent upon, statewide coordinating boards, the legislature, or other agents of public control in the exercise of these functions. Once named, private boards with rare exceptions enjoy full formal authority, though some have in practice been subordinate to other authorities, as in the case of some denominational colleges.

The makeup of the previously discussed constituencies represented in campus governance is determined by their roles; e.g., student, faculty, or administrator. With trustees, it is appropriate to ask: Are trustees to be viewed as constituencies in the sense that applies to these other groups? Who should be considered for the position of trustee? To answer that question, it is helpful to review the functions of trustees, the present makeup of trustee bodies, and the recent changes of circumstance which have a bearing upon the appropriate makeup of campus governing boards.

In 1968-69 Morton Rauh did the first comprehensive survey of the makeup of campus boards of trustees in the United States and inquired as to their work and their attitudes as trustees.[6] As disclosed in the survey, the actual work of trustees is less concentrated in the functions just listed (choice of mission and of president and monitoring of overall effectiveness) than in matters of finance, plant, and fund raising (pp. 189-90). In a college with an unquestioned mission and a strikingly successful president, it may well be that the most critical functions of the trustees call for relatively little of their time. In these respects their task is to stand by for the time of need. Moreover, a small

---

[6] Rauh, then Vice-President for Finance of Antioch College, was supported in his study by the Sloan Foundation, by a grant from the Campus Governance Program of the American Association for Higher Education, by Antioch College, and by the in-kind contribution of staff and other assistance from the Educational Testing Service of Princeton, New Jersey. Rodney Hartnett was his principal collaborator. See the list of publications in Appendix A for their reports.

college often cannot afford all of the staff it needs, much less the quality of staff it can obtain as a contributed service through its board. However, the minimal board time given to purpose and effectiveness may be less a function of need than of the interests and capabilities of the preponderant membership.

Fault can be found with typical practice on two counts. One is the inadequate attention given to the distinction between the role of trustees as a board and the managerial services which particular members or groups may render. If the trustees' activity in finance, plant development and management, and fund raising goes beyond evaluation of performance and counsel to the actual conduct of the managerial functions, this is likely to cause their preoccupations with that activity to carry undue weight in their deliberations.

The second skeptical question to direct at present trustee practices points to the crisis in campus governance which prompted this study. Insofar as the conflicts on campus betray questions of confidence in the purposes and leadership of a campus, the conflicts go to the heart of trustee responsibilities. The conflict is no less serious if it is peaceful and nonviolent, or if it is expressed in substantial apathy rather than noisy demonstrations. Indeed, the growing revolt of taxpayers and tuition payers over the cost of higher education may be a more important indicator of this crisis than any disturbances on campus, and may be much less important as a question of financing strategy than as a question of public trust in the purposes and effectiveness of colleges and universities. To put the point differently, the flagging willingness to pay is an indicator which links the problems of purpose and financing, institutional priorities and public support. This linkage and its current weakness, rather than concerns such as gift campaigns, should be high on the agendas of both private and public college trustees.

The demand for higher education has never been greater than today. Yet the financing of both public and private colleges has much of the air of a mendicant operation. Why must those who render such a crucial service beg for resources to meet its costs? What alternatives are feasible in our society? These are questions for trustee resolution and action. A consideration of illustrative trends in the society will suggest the urgency and complexity of these questions.

Americans have been largely ignorant of the true costs of higher education and have expected much of them to be borne by charity. This expectation could be met as long as college students were largely an economic elite and few in number, professors were poorly paid, and the generation and transmission of knowledge did not require expensive technology. All of these conditions are rapidly changing. The sheer increase in numbers enrolled, the rising proportion of low-income students, the increased professionalization of faculty, and the escalating technology of the "knowledge industry" are now commonplace. In part the enrollment changes reflect a fashion. But behind the fashion are two kinds of needs that will persist: the need of the individual for the power and advancement which greater learning can give him, and the need of the society for the improved quality of life and effectiveness in pursuing social purposes which cannot be achieved without a greater call upon higher education.

Both the individual and the society will find this new knowledge a double-edged sword. For the things already wanted, knowledge helps get more for less cost. But part of the cost of the technological gains brought by knowledge is side effects upon the life of the individual and the society. For example, a person earns more after he has his degree; this enables him to eat more and do less physical work; this combination makes him fat and less healthy, etc. Or, to illustrate an analogous social change, knowledge enables us to move faster and further with less cost by cars and planes. Cars and planes pollute the atmosphere, cut up communities with thruways, raise taxes for highways, contribute to the bankruptcy of railroads, etc.

A potential benefit of higher education is the contribution it can make to both the individual and society in designing new ways of living that avert or minimize unwanted side effects. To gain this benefit, however, requires consideration of the fact that these changes in costs and benefits affect different people in different degrees at different times. This introduces problems. While some people get higher salaries and better jobs with more education and technological progress, others gain less, lose their jobs, or have their property deteriorate in value as the technological changes transform the inner cities into slums. There are two types of bad effects here. First, creation of slums ultimately hurts nearly everyone, and most will agree to attack this problem. Again, however, the mode of attack will put costs on different people in different degrees. The choice of attack then creates the second type of problem, which was also present in the first round of ill effects: a problem of equity in sharing the benefits and bearing the costs of an increasingly productive society. The knowledge which higher education generates and disseminates bears upon both types of problem. The choice as to what kinds of knowledge are sought and disseminated and in whose interests becomes a critical choice, with political and ethical as well as economic and cultural significance. In this choice will students, faculty, and the university or its departments be nonpartisan, indifferent, neutral, or uninvolved?

Nonpartisanship, noninvolvement, indifference, and neutrality are not the same. To be neutral is to take no side, whatever the merits of the cases. To be indifferent is not to care, whereas a neutral may care but feel obliged not to intervene. One may be uninvolved because he is unaware, is partisan but feels powerless, or does not care. To be nonpartisan is not necessarily to remain neutral, but to decide and act on the merits of the case without yielding to the special interests of one's political allies, or weighing the effect upon political enemies, or becoming captive of the assumptions of disputing parties. In the past colleges and universities have been expected generally to be neutral, except about ignorance, their own survival, academic freedom, and matters of the founders' doctrine. Lately, students and faculty, as citizens and individuals, have acted with increasing frequency as partisans in issues of public policy. They have done so on the basis of constitutional rights. In the case of faculty, the advocacy has often extended, as a matter of professional rights, to their judgment as experts, when they were expressing judgments consistent with professional standards in the area of their expertise.

Since at least the time of the Morrill Act, however, colleges have been increasingly expected to serve the public interest by engaging in projects which in effect change practices or reconstitute occupations and institutions of society. Agriculture has been radically transformed by the partnership of government and higher education in bringing knowledge to bear upon farming. This intervention has hardly been a case of noninvolvement or neutrality as to whose interests were affected or which features of American agricultural institutions were replaced. Small farming has been drastically curtailed in significance. Literally millions of people have moved from farm to city. Those who could organize to capture agricultural expertise and use it on a large scale have profited disproportionately.

Urban practices and institutions now call for a similarly radical change. Should this change be as subject to disproportionate exploitation by different interests as was the change of rural life? In the case of the revolution in agriculture, no one really planned a revolution. It occurred inadvertently as a by-product of getting more for less. We can hardly be so naïve about urban change today. People on campuses know this, and some of them are better organized than others to exploit the knowledge campuses can develop. If this knowledge is to be used to evoke a better planned effort at social renewal, the urban revolution of the late twentieth century will differ from the rural one of the late nineteenth century in that it will result from a competition of new conceptions as to the best possible direction the future might take. And this will be a competition of visions of the good, not merely the competition of different suppliers to do the same job. In this competition the decision as to the control of university and college resources and efforts will be a deadly serious, high priority, political decision.

In this context higher education can scarcely go on pretending to be indifferent or uninvolved. Its institutions, as a demand of inquiry, could be the society's best practitioners of nonpartisanship, but hardly of neutrality.

The campus will be a "hot spot" for another reason in the upcoming decades. The enterprise of higher education has become a much larger part of the economic activity of the nation than it was before 1900. If appropriate national concerns receive priority, this relative growth might continue. Such a growth "industry" demands enormous resources. In doing so, it competes for scarce national resources with the military enterprise, with industrial enterprise seeking various forms of direct and indirect governmental help (e.g., the transportation industry), and with such sectors of the economy as the social welfare enterprise. Like other potential competitors, institutions of higher education may collude with those of the military or industry to serve one another in ways that do not serve the rest of the society ideally. Such collusion may even be to the detriment of the overall enterprise whose participants engage in the collusion. Thus some colleges are accused of selling their birthright of intellectual freedom for the mess of defense pottage available in classified research contracts. The cry is raised with a serious show of feasibility that the aggregate demands of the military are incompatible with that magnitude of development of higher education which is essential to national strength and thus to national security. It is further charged, even among nonpacifists, that war itself is not compatible with optimum worldwide economic and social development and is thus counterproductive as a social institution and inimical to the survival of freely inquiring institutions of higher education.

Controversies over these issues are almost certain to grow in the upcoming decades. They will not ease the tasks of managing college–community relations or of mustering the needed financial support for higher education. Yet the integrity of higher education and its utility to society require that the controversies rage.

The examples given here could be multiplied many times. The work ethic of our former economy of scarcity produces an emerging society of voluntary leisure in the suburbs and enforced leisure in the slums, and some campuses become a microcosm in which the clash of values reaches sharpest articulation. A society which has favored producers with advantages for capital formation and profit making now faces an emerging society of consumers in search of Naders to raid their exploiters with the weapons of investigation and dissemination—matters in which the campuses have potentially important resources. A society which has taken pride in large families and has long given homage to the nuclear family is faced with the population bomb and a new sexual freedom, and again the controversy is spoken of, as well as acted out, on some campuses and carefully avoided on others. A society still deeply imbued with the residues of racial prejudice and discrimination confronts more and more campuses which make it a matter of cultural mission to press for polycultural equality.

Nor are the campuses always a progressive force and the society conservative. Patterns of accreditation and certification thwart the needs of disadvantaged individuals for rapid, precisely designed means of increasing their work and living opportunities through education. An increasingly educated society is learning to be skeptical of the iconoclasm of campuses which attack the traditions and institutions of the society without applying a similar critique to their own myths and dogmas. A leisure-oriented campus encounters users who cannot afford to pay for an enterprise which fails to find ways to gain greater productivity from its professionals. An increasingly self-respecting segment of less verbal citizens encounter high-verbal campuses which do not embody respect for the varieties of competence and intellectuality not measured by word skills and number skills. In this matter of conflicts, campus–community relations will change because of changes in the character of society's need for higher education.

The importance of knowledge to future society will consist less and less in its utility for implementing chosen social values, institutions, and practices. Because of the complexity of possibilities and problems of society, campuses will be increasingly needed to participate in reshaping institutions, policies, and programs. The campuses will be less and less able to shield themselves by attributing the critiques of society to individual professors and students, for the department or institute or task force of campus people will be doing their social experiments as agents of the university or college. The sheer size and complexity of problems for research and experiment will require team effort on an institutional scale.

In the past universities, when engaged in controversial social or scientific ventures, have protected their flanks by performing at the same time a large amount of noncontroversial public service and training. These activities are likely in the future to become increasingly a function of a growing noncampus educational "force." This noncampus educational force consists of training and intellectual services provided by industries (General Motors Institute, for example), federal programs contracted out to private entrepreneurs organized specifically for such work, municipal or state agencies created to use federal funds for similar work, public service television, proprietary training schools, etc. A recent study estimates this noncampus educational force will increase its enrollment from about 17.3 million per year in 1940 (including duplications) to 82.4 million by 1975, with 60.3 already reached in 1970 and the numerical increases rising year by year. These enrollments will soon be ten times those of campuses. They do not represent ten times the educational work, because they are largely part-time activities, but the political significance of the numbers may be more closely related to the enrollments than to the work.[7]

The social need for higher education has been stressed in this discussion of the causes and reasons for change in campus–community relations. Higher education also needs the collabora-

---

[7] Stanley Moses. "Notes on the Learning Force," *Notes on the Future of Education* 7: 6-8; January-February 1970.

tion of others, who must finance it. Unless they believe in it, they will not use it, and colleges will wither or weaken from disuse. Also, the life and institutions of society are playing an increasing role as realties in which students and professors engage as the subject matter of their studies. This change is not merely a matter of pedagogical changes involving an increased use of travel, television, work, and other means of firsthand engagement with the world of today. It is also a product of growing relative emphasis upon the arts, the humanities, and the social sciences, and an apparent tendency in all of these areas to put increasing emphasis upon the present and future as against the past. As the social sciences become increasingly sophisticated and powerful in their research methods, they depend upon increasingly extensive access to the day-to-day activities of the people and institutions they study. The pace of growth of knowledge and the rate of change in society also make for the investment of greater energy in direct interactions with the contemporary world as a condition of both effective research and effective teaching.

Our changing wants interact with our changing ways of getting them to produce a growing interdependence between higher education and other activities and institutions of society. That interdependence is a key to the lost consensus on campus and to a crisis in public confidence in higher education. It provides a context in which trustee attention is urgently needed for the overall issues of purpose, priority, design of campus–community relations, and rationalization of the choices on those relations with the mode of financing of the institution.

The actual makeup of boards of trustees is not related well to this recommended task at all. For example, trustees are occupationally atypical of the types of expertness that are relevant to the problems just outlined. They are heavily concentrated in manufacturing, money management, and law, and enjoy high incomes (median between $30,000 and $49,000 per year), which are a mark of success of a kind. While not all high earners share one another's biases, and good income need be no disqualification in itself, the proportion of wealthy trustees is likely to deprive a board of the mix of perspective and of urgency appropriate to some of the issues just outlined. In a society facing urgent problems of racial justice, in which higher education should be an example of good practice, the proportion of Negro trustees is only 1.3 percent in the aggregate and is not evenly distributed among types of institutions. Age brings experience and often marks continuity of service and high competence in a calling, but 88 percent of trustees in 1968 were over fifty years old. A larger infusion of younger members could again diversify trustee perspectives, help in their communications with youth, and preserve a better balance of new life and developing leadership. Trustees are also typically male (86 percent) in a society still struggling to enfranchise the female majority. Even in religious affiliation (75 percent Protestant), after allowance is made for the special distributions of trustees by religion on denominationally sponsored campuses, the trustees are not typical of the public they serve. In race, religion, occupation, and income, the trustees of selective institutions are even less typical than those of others.[8]

Still different problems of makeup emerge when particular boards or types of boards of trustees are studied. A quiet revolution has developed within the last decade in the change of Catholic college boards from clerical to lay control. A number of community colleges formerly governed by boards for lower schools now have separate and differently constituted boards. As mentioned already, some states have recently subordinated the formerly independent boards of individual campuses to a statewide authority or required certain forms of statewide coordination which have the effect of changing the composition as well as the prerogatives of controlling boards. Negro college boards which were formerly dominated by white trustees in a position to help have adjusted their membership to changed perceptions of who can help and who can best define the proper functions and interests of those institutions.

It is, of course, not important that trustees be typical in some of these respects. Those who protect the public interest in governing need not be altogether typical of the public they protect. The constituencies should have effective advocacy before, and response from, the board; they need not be, and cannot always be, equally well represented on the board. Moreover, the complexity and novelty of contemporary problems of campus governance might well be best met by new divisions of labor and new methods of empowering the constituencies. Three examples, related to the faculty, students, and the community respectively, will illustrate the possibilities.

---

8 Rauh, 17, pp. 170-76.

A typical board of trustees is minimally involved in academic and student affairs. A recent exception, the reversal of a faculty appointment by the University of California regents, "earned some sort of prize for the most inappropriate action of the year," according to Morton Rauh.[9] Yet while a board should not intrude upon management and professional functions, either academic or financial, how can it monitor the work of a campus without major attention to, and competence in, academic affairs if the preponderant public interest in that campus is in the perform-ance of intellectual services?

The faculty are a natural resource for the trustee function of evaluating institutional performance of this public interest. As professionals, the faculty hold the intellectual life as their peculiar concern and trust. In the British and Canadian systems of cam-pus governance, this fact is recognized in the dominant role of faculty in governing boards. In these systems the purse-strings are watched by government as well as by the governing boards. In the United States where finance and other resources are more fully controlled at board level, the pecuniary and personnel inter-ests of faculty have acted as barriers to their direct participation on boards.

In addition, the tradition in the United States has recognized that values other than the intellectual enter into the choice of institutional purposes and task. Lay control has existed in part to see that these other values—whether religion, national purpose, pedagogy, or ideology—were chosen according to the sponsors' lights. Perhaps, then, other means must be found in the United States for bringing educational expertise into, or to the disposal of, trustee bodies. One such device is the provision for the faculty or a campus senate to select a portion of the members of the board or, in public systems, for a qualified panel of educators to nominate candidates for the choice of the public appointing authority.

When Princeton University announced that a graduated senior would now regularly be named to its board of trustees, Rauh objected on multiple grounds: The presence of students as board members may tempt the board to inject itself into actions it is not competent to take and should keep delegated to management. In any case one or two or three students cannot represent the range of views held by students, especially with the rapid shifts

---

[9] Rauh, 19, pp. 1-2.

of concern typical today. Worst of all, the appointment of students as trustees may "fool some people into thinking that student aspirations are being met by a move that at best is but a token of good intentions." Rauh suggests more powerful and practical modes of enfranchisement: requiring boards to meet publicly where students and other constituents may attend, empowering students as well as faculty to select some of the trustees, focusing agenda upon issues vital to student concerns (e.g., the roles of students and faculty in determining curricular policies), and allowing students to participate as working members in task groups or committees which shape the resolutions coming to the board for action. "It is sheer fantasy," says Rauh, "to think that a change as superficial as giving the student a token seat on the board of trustees will satisfy his aspirations for influence, participation, and, above all, some measure of control over his own education." [10]

The case of representation of the immediate and more remote communities concerned with a campus is even more difficult in theory, if not in practice. In the past community relations have been largely left to trustees and administrators except when the outside world threatened intervention on campus. The attitude underlying this assignment of functions is changing. On some campuses it is already a matter of policy to confer and collaborate actively with representatives of the community about the educational services the campus should render. This applies particularly to community and state colleges. On city campuses today it is becoming increasingly essential to confer with neighbors before expanding facilities or undertaking programs with a direct impact upon the neighborhood. But the change to which we refer is more fundamental. It is one toward active interest in collaborative planning and continuous communication with a view to finding the most appropriate response to the emerging interdependence of campus and community.

This change of attitude or philosophy will generally involve the consideration of new mechanisms. These may include changes in membership of the campus trustees and will surely include new arrangements for communication and joint problem definition and problem solving. They should in many cases include an attempt to understand with greater precision who are the constituencies on and off campus whose interests and concerns are

---

[10] *Ibid.*, p. 7.

most vitally affected by the choice among options as to how campus and community interact. It will no longer do to assume that an appointed public board ensures effective representation or advocacy for community constituencies.

For the system of higher education as a whole, diversity and decentralization of control will be of increasingly critical importance at the very time when they are increasingly difficult to achieve. The financing of private and public colleges and universities is becoming less and less distinct as public universities mount large fund-raising efforts among private sources, and private colleges turn increasingly to federal and state subsidies to avoid pricing students out of their market. There is an inevitable pressure from funding sources to impose at least minimal definition and monitoring upon the use of their funds. In times of political crisis and controversy, that pressure often touches upon the very freedom of inquiry and teaching. If added to these financial pressures is a more intimate pattern of communication to cope with the increasing interdependency of campus and community, the result could be a further subtle and pervasive blanket of constraint upon intellectual freedom. A pressure for homogenization not unlike that besetting secondary and elementary education could plague higher education.

Interdependence need not produce such unwanted change. Given the variety of subcultures in our society, the diversity of interests and concerns, and the degree of commitment to political and constitutional freedoms, a closer interaction of campus and communities could produce a new variety in the functions and styles of American campuses. The possibility of creating within higher education a new relevance to social need and a renewal of intellectual potency should preoccupy the boards of trustees as they address the changes now in store.

REALIGNMENT OF AUTHORITY ON CAMPUS

The tasks and trends confronting those who govern campuses dictate the need for a new sophistication in the design of governing structures and processes, but they do not dictate any one solution that will serve for all campuses. What can be proposed is criteria to be heeded by particular campuses and types of campuses in the design of their own authority structures. The following statements summarize criteria implicit as assumptions or proposals in the preceding discussion.

1. The authority structure should reflect a genuine commitment to enfranchise constituencies previously unrepresented or underrepresented. This principle does not imply direct participation of particular constituents in the board of turstees, but it does require arrangements which provide for effective advocacy for, and response to, their concerns.

2. The processes and prerogatives in governing should be designed to foster the cooperation of each constituency and to further the contributions for which it has special competence. At the same time the pattern of sharing authority should avoid any undue effects of the special interests and disadvantages which the different constituencies bring with their roles.

3. The system of governance of a campus should provide for a division of labor between policy making and managing, and between the board of trustees and other councils and committees. The system should provide effective means for constituencies to be heard and heeded at the level and locus where their particular concerns receive final disposition. In state systems and private institutions with multiple campuses this principle calls for mechanisms for these campuses and their constituencies to be heard at the statewide or systemwide level.

4. The existence of diverse constituencies with often conflicting interests and perspectives need not imply that all fundamental policy making become a process of group negotiation—of collective bargaining, compromise, and accommodation. At the same time, not every issue can be settled on rationally persuasive grounds in the eyes of every constituency. To reduce the frequency of impasse and to minimize damage from it, the system of governance should provide mechanisms of accommodation short of coercion and violence. The enfranchisement recommended in Criterion 1 should result in purposes and priorities which will reflect constituency concerns and minimize the likelihood of coercive confrontations.

5. The rapidity of external and internal changes affecting campuses requires processes of governance which are more flexible in everyday operation, capable of more rapid and effective response to crisis, and less cumbersome to change in response to new working agreements than have been typical in the past.

The implementation of these principles will affect substantially the concepts and practices with regard to consent, accountability, and leadership. These implications are explored in Chapter 3. Much of their meaning, however, can best be seen if the variety of problems, perspectives, and contexts of governance is clearly in view. Extracts from the Campus Governance Program's findings on these matters are reported in Chapter 2.

What the Campus Constituencies See and Say

2

CONSTITUENTS' PERCEPTIONS FALL INTO COMPLEX PATTERNS. The constituent groups share some concerns, differ on others, and differ substantially in the concerns they share from campus to campus. The problems of effective governance are correspondingly diverse. Although in theory the functions of governing may be the same among these diverse situations, the practical task of conceiving and achieving effectiveness on a particular campus requires a knowledge of its specific concerns and practices. In this chapter highlights from the reports of constituents are sketched. Each of the ten highlights selected was chosen for the speculations it prompts about governance problems. For their meaning to be clear, it will be necessary to interject at intervals some explanation of how data were obtained. In the first highlight, however, this explanation is deferred in order to convey a sense of the scene of the studies.

HIGHLIGHT 1. PROBLEMS IN GOVERNING A PUBLIC UNIVERSITY

The governing and managing of a campus resist understanding because they are so complex. The Campus Governance Program sought to abstract from this complexity some key features of campus life on a few campuses in the hope that their significant interrelations for governing would begin to show. The full meaning of the data here reported is perhaps best seen when the "hard data" of statistically treated studies are combined with the "soft data" of interviews and impressions to create a sense of the whole scene on a particular campus. University B afforded a suitable array of data for this purpose. The vignette which follows is, however graphic, still an abstraction. It must be viewed as a complex hypothesis, reconstructing the features of the actual campus with a combination of data and speculation.

A Midwestern University in the Making

University B (UB) in 1967–68 was a campus in transition. It had had only 6,200 students in 1959; now its enrollment was nearing 13,500. Long a state teachers college, it had just achieved university status. With 85 percent of its students still majoring in teacher education, its faculty was changing to one of many departments and disciplines, with more research interests and less concern with public service to schools and communities. Still unselective in admissions and drawing students almost entirely from its midwestern neighborhood, it nevertheless had students with distinctly greater intellectual and expressive needs than a decade ago. However, its climate was largely unchanged in its vocational and collegiate orientation. While the university was changing in many fundamental ways, the immediate community and the state legislature held expectations that were less changed. For twenty-three years, since the end of World War II, UB had been led by the same dynamic president. Now he was retiring.

Size, mission, students, program, faculty, and president— all of these were being changed in 1967–68. Change was also under way in the methods of coping both with the ongoing life and activities of the campus and with these major changes. Changes in governing and managing, however, were harder to see and to chart. It was easy to pinpoint tensions, but not to diagnose their causes or conceive what those responsible should do.

A sketch of the presidency, the University Senate, and reported campus concerns and climate reflect the condition and problems of governing and managing this campus.

The Presidency

The university history is unabashed in its Horatio Alger image of the retiring president's life and career. Of humble origins, he

believed in hard work: "made it through college the hard way."
He planned ahead, read "voraciously," believed in self-improve-
ment: "Most everything I've done, I've done in order to be able
to do something else better." He was "handsome, vigorous, de-
cisive, and enthusiastic." It was no accident that he had led the
teachers college to become a state university. He thought big
("makes no little plans"), was a great competitor ("plays to
win"), and was ever optimistic. "I prefer to see the world in
terms of challenges, not problems," he told his interviewers. His
origins were respectable ("Theirs was the busy, happy but hectic
life, rich in all but money") and religious ("You know, there's
something in Wesleyan Methodism that says if you believe you
are right, you can do what you should"). He shared the egali-
tarian dream, and realized it. "When he became president (of the
college), he was no longer the 'country kid' he has reason to
remember. He was an educational administrator of wide experience, determined and happily able to 'keep on top' of the difficult
and varied duties of a college president." Seven pages of the
catalog were devoted to his vignette, and two pages to the philosophy of the university and the changing future of education.

No one questioned that the president had been effective in
areas of his concern. How he did so, what the effects of his style
were, and how these should be appraised were matters of much
less agreement. Some viewed his work as a heroic victory against
long odds; others as an autocratic, manipulative use of power
and relationships to gain prestige for the campus at the price
of mediocrity.

Faculty critics had varied concerns: "It sometimes seems
that anything that would provide difficulty is pushed aside."
"There is a tendency to gloss things over, especially on the part
of the president." The English Department, another faculty
member stated, was unable to get a change of department head
because the president simply said the head was permanent. Major
administrators perceived the president as doing the hiring, controlling the budget, doing a minimum of delegating authority,
consulting little, communicating primarily with the vice-presidents but not with the faculty, often glossing over problems and
issues, but functioning clearly as the last resort in problems.
Faculty also perceived the president as holder of the purse-strings.
One complained that the president was cut off from knowledge
of what the departments needed, and they and the middle ad-

ministrators were cut off from knowledge and voice in financial matters.

The president stressed cooperation of the college with the community and prided himself on warm "town–gown relations." Some faculty reported that this emphasis worked to the detriment of the intellectual climate of the campus: the president, they said, saw his strength in community support, local and statewide, and was anxious to avoid confrontations and controversial events. He "behaves like a school principal, keeping tight control," charged a critic.

The president also prided himself on having a friendly campus. His own style reflected this concern. Those who defended his work, though a minority of the interviewees, said that the administration was always willing to sit down and talk, was liberal in its responses, catered to students' needs, and did not hide or avoid problems. One faculty member reported that he had had no problems he had been unable to resolve. Once when the "usual routes" denied his wish to teach a course, he wrote to the president, and they "worked it out." "The president's open door is truly real," he added.

The majority of students interviewed were critical of the administration. The student government president called the university administration "weak, ineffectual, do-nothing, back-stabbing" and added that most faculty and students were afraid of administrators and distrusted them. Students, he said, were "heard from more often" than faculty but had no real power. Another student moaned about the "administration's hold over everything" and cited the case of a professor who was accused of improper relations with his co-ed students, sought an open hearing without success, and "finally was forced to resign."

A perspective on these reactions to the president's style is afforded by the 342 responses on the Pre-Interview Questionnaire to questions as to whom the respondent would see to get information or to get something done in the area of his primary concern. The vice-president for academic affairs was most nominated for getting information (98 mentions) and the president was second (35 mentions). The two tied for most mentions (75 each) for the one to see to get action. The total mentions for getting information and action were 173 and 110 respectively for the vice-president and the president, with the dean of the teachers college a distant third with 46 mentions. Of the top fifteen persons named, only one was a student, viz., the president of the student body, with 19 mentions. This highly concentrated pattern of information holding and influence evoked interview comments stressing that "regular channels" must be used to learn things or to get action and that accessibility becomes difficult as an inquirer is referred to "the higher ups." In the data on campus cultures the campus emerged as high on institutional self-maintenance and impulse control. In some cases, interviewees did think that the vice-president for academic affairs had become "more useful" in the last year as "the president has become a lame duck"; for example, budget information and decisions could be obtained which earlier would have been referred upward. On the other hand, several students cited a "talk in" to discuss student complaints at which, they alleged, not a faculty member or administrator "showed." Even when a committee was set up to investigate a problem and the complaints were heard, students expected the committee not to act and expected one of the administrators to act instead, perhaps without consulting the committee.

For all of these difficulties and complaints, University B was not a campus in turmoil. The graph of its reporting of problems in Exhibit 2 (pages 56-57) shows a campus which, compared with others of similar size and control, was not vocal or agitated. The sense of institutional achievement under the retiring president was generally shared and seen as a source of pride, though the impending change of presidents had made for some slowdown in decision making, a sense of lost momentum or direction, and a resulting apathy.

Linked to the uncertainty caused by one president's leaving was that caused by another's coming. This was accentuated by the way UB's new president was selected—the policies and style of communication about the process of selection, and its result. Most of the sixty interviewees did not know what qualifications the presidential selection committee had sought in a new president, nor what qualifications the appointee had. One faculty member attributed this ignorance to apathy: "People do not care." In any event the selection committee was reported to be unanimous, but the campus community was without a sense of consensus at the time of the interviews. No students had served on the selection committee, but some faculty had participated actively in its work.

The missing consensus bore not only upon the choice of president, but also upon the purpose and portent of the choice. Some were excited that the new president wanted the University "to be the faculty's"—an allusion to the perception of the retiring president as autocratic and too ready to kowtow to the legislature. Others feared that "the new man" would "not be as strong a leader" as his predecessor and would be "overwhelmed by the University Senate." Still others feared that the incoming president would "rock the boat." In a university growing so rapidly, it would have been difficult enough to get a sense of agreement in any case, but the interviewees conveyed an impression that preoccupation with the selection had quite overshadowed the need for constituency support of the process and its outcome.

The University Senate

Running through many specific concerns expressed at University B was a more general one about the place of "educationists" and teacher education in its future. As one administrator remarked, the science and humanities faculty resented "the teacher education orientation" which had dominated the campus and caused undersupport of science and the humanities. This resentment seemed to have been a factor in the movement in 1962 to form a University Senate, along with the need for new structures for faculty voice as the University grew in size and complexity. Some of the resentful faculty felt that in the Senate the educationists formed a special interest group, with disproportionate power because all major administrators came from the "trade of education." Several faculty members felt that educationists gained power by their cohesiveness and organization, in contrast with other faculty groups which felt differently and acted competitively even though under one dean.

The structure of the Senate lent itself to a linking of dissent about a centralized administration and a dominant faculty of teacher educators. The Senate consisted of 100 full professors (in 1967-68), 14 administrators named by virtue of other positions, and 43 elected representatives. The administrators included the president, his executive assistant, the vice-presidents, and the full deans of instructional affairs. The elected members consisted of one elected representative for every twenty faculty members (other than those already members of the Senate) and one for every twenty professional members of four administrative

units (Instructional Affairs, Student Affairs, Public Affairs, and
Business Affairs). A year before the Campus Governance Program visit there had been a reorganization of the Senate, and
students were invited for the first time to attend and participate
in actions of the Senate and its committees. One faculty member
commented that the students who had participated were prepared
and responsible. The University Senate, however, was rarely
mentioned by students. Their interest focused upon the Student
Senate, whose recommendations had to go through the University
Senate.

The University Senate was seen by several interviewees as
providing a modicum of faculty autonomy and "the only check"
on the president's power. "The most dramatic change (in a
decade) has been the emergence of the Senate," said one. Yet the
overwhelming majority of interviewees regarded its authority as
questionable and felt that it was beleaguered by trivial problems.

The criticisms of the Senate showed a large gap between
expectations and performance, but the expectations themselves
were sometimes in conflict. The Senate, said some who were
critical of the administration's priorities, "doesn't really reflect
institutional concern"; others complained that "it tends to revolt
against authority." A number of interviewees feared a developing Senate oligarchy: "In the name of democracy, it controls
what changes are made." "The vocal minority control the proceedings." "It's too heavily weighted with full professors." A
number of complaints centered on the procedures of the Senate.
A faculty member who had recently become a professor thought
the Senate a waste of time, fussing about petty details which
should have been left to administrators. Another noted its difficulties in getting a quorum.

Much criticism of the Senate focused on its "committee problem." By policy, the Senate set up committees to study problems
presented for its action. Most who commented on these committees criticized them for the ratio of effort to output and for
their sheer number. "We are," explained one faculty member,
"bogged down with committees campus-wide and don't have a
chance to prepare our lessons." He was then on "three college-
wide committees, two ad hoc committees, and two others." Another commented that this could never be a research university
if the faculty were to take time for both committee work and
teaching. Two of the most frequent complaints about committees

were that their decisions were ignored or bypassed later and that they tended to deal with "petty aspects of a problem without knowing the whole." A few faculty members, reacting to the over-all situation, said they were "generally pleased with the course of events, but distressed because of the time spent on matters with no knowledge of results."

Although in the interviews faculty members tended to view themselves as relatively impotent in governance and overburdened (by their own fault) with administrative "odds and ends," the returns from the Pre-Interview Questionnaire showed a normal to low frequency of problems reported.[1] Judging by the number of specific problem areas checked by at least 30 percent of one or another of the role groups, the educational milieu was the area of most frequent concern. Least concern was indicated about control of the academic program and control of social and political behavior. Of intermediate frequency were reports about problems of resources. This ordering is different from that for all campuses combined; there physical and financial resources came first, and the control of social and political behavior second. For UB, however, the ordering is congruent with other data obtained in the Campus Governance Program which showed a greater need for intellectual stimulus than the reported "press" of the institutional environment in that direction. On problem checking, for example, students emphasized problems about the relevance of their courses to their needs, the adequacy of teaching, advising, and counseling, and the quality of the faculty. Faculty, on the other hand, showed most frequent concern about teaching loads, time for research, and the quality of students.

The picture of University B derived from the Activities Index and College Characteristics Index reinforces the image of mis-placed effort on the part of Senate and administration. The cul-ture students experience encourages them toward the vocational and collegiate. For students who study constantly and allow themselves little fun, this press might be appropriate; but the students here, particularly the men, express a need for the in-tellectual and the expressive and find the institutional inputs working in the opposite direction. Within the past decade, the institution has actually hardened its pattern of institutional main-tenance, impulse control, and stress on vocationalism. The prin-

---

[1] These data were summarized and analyzed by Dr. Ruth Churchill, Antioch College.

cipal countervailing change has been the change in entering
students, and only the male students show this increased collegiate, expressive, and intellectual input at a significant level. There
is also another important change among students. They are more
heterogeneous than a decade ago, with more collegiate than protective needs on balance, but there is a greater scatter of students
among different types than before.[2]

How do these changes in campus climate translate into
problems for governance? One hypothesis to account for the data
would be that the preoccupation of faculty and administrative
leaders with university status, academic prestige, and community
acceptability have diverted their energies from the tasks of
adjusting to the intellectual and expressive needs of their changing students. Curiously, response to these student needs would
have made for a climate more supportive of high quality research,
but it would have diverted energies from the work of publication
and the mustering of resources which are the normal stigmata of
university prestige. To bring itself into a position of coherent
effort to perform an intellectual service compatible with its
makeup, UB was seeking, as the new administration took
over, to build a stronger collaboration of faculty and administration, to arrest its rate of growth, to be selective in its expansion
of graduate programs, and to put special effort into the improvement of teaching and the strengthening of the intellectual stimuli
on campus. It was far from clear, however, if the forces essential
to these results could be mustered in sufficient strength to prevail.

A Warning to Readers

No two campuses present the same picture. When subjected to
common inquiries, however, they have common features and instructive differences. We turn now to this type of findings. In
doing so, we offer a suggestion—"warning" may be a better
word—to readers.

Those who are willing to enjoy recommendations before labor-
ing through the evidence are urged to read Chapter 3 before
reading the remainder of Chapter 2. The data and analysis of the
remainder of Chapter 2 are, for all of our effort, the hardest
reading in this book.

---

[2] The terms "vocational," "collegiate," "intellectual," "expressive," and
"protective" are defined on pp. 91 and 92.

HIGHLIGHT 2. WHEN A NONPROBLEM IS A PROBLEM [3]

In this chapter data from the Activities Index (AI), College Characteristics Index (CCI), and the Pre-Interview Questionnaire (PIQ) of the Nineteen Campus Study are stressed. In some cases these data are compared or combined with information from other sources, for example, interviews from this same Study, documents, the College Trustee Questionnaire, interviews of the Task Force on Faculty Representation, and other reports in the literature. The data newly generated by the Campus Governance Program are shown in Table 1.

Table 1. New data generated by the Campus Governance Program

Instrument	Nature of material	Quantity of responses
Pre-Interview Questionnaire	Problem areas, who has information, who gets things done	3,278 usable replies
Activities Index	What respondents prefer to do and to experience, as clues to their psycho-social *needs*	1,109 new replies
College Characteristics Index	What respondents perceive as existing or going on, as clues to the climate or press of the institutional environment	1,058 new replies
Interview Schedule of Nineteen Campuses	How the campus copes with its problems	903 interviews of one or more hours
College Trustee Questionnaire	Who trustees are, what they do as trustees, how they think about higher education	5,180 returns, 536 institutions
Task Force Interviews on Faculty Representation	Nature and causes of faculty unrest and recommendations on the authority faculty should have	Interviews on 35 campuses

The governing of a campus can be viewed as a process of coping with its problems and opportunities to achieve effectiveness in its purposes. In this effort diverse persons interact in multiple roles within a distinctive climate and organization to

---

[3] The research on reported campus problems was directed by Stephen Plumer. The major summary, from which these highlights are drawn, was prepared by Suzanne Imes under the supervision of Stephen Plumer and Michael Metty.

perform their respective functions. There is constant change of
persons, roles, climate, organization, and functions. One practical
way to throw light upon this very involved process is to gather
reports of diverse participants as to what the problems and priorities are, and how they are coped with. With these responses one
can then construct a coherent description and explanation of the
campus' process and problems of governing. The accounts of
different campuses can then be compared to investigate comparative problems of governance. The Campus Governance Program
staff divided the data gathering between written responses to
questionnaires (PIQ, AI, CCI) and interviews in order to get the
best use of time and resources in this inquiry. The interviews
began with individuals whom the questionnaire returns screened
out as key informants and with issues pointed up by the questionnaire returns.

Exhibit 1 shows the complete list of 120 problem areas presented to respondents in the PIQ. This list resulted from the
following assumption:

> Life and work in a college can be represented in
> terms of four dimensions—intellectual climate, aca-
> demic program, student life, and working conditions.
> These four dimensions are affected by the interactions
> of the people in the institution with the available re-
> sources and the policies and procedures governing the
> ways in which they go about their daily work. The
> unique outcome of these interactions distinguishes one
> campus from another. (Introduction to the Question-
> naire)

Charting the four dimensions against the three variables of people, resources, and policies and procedures yielded twelve boxes,
into each of which ten illustrative problem areas were put. The
respondent could add items in a thirteenth box.

The focus of this questionnaire upon problem areas both
reflects the purpose of the study and points up one of its limitations. The purpose of the investigators was to locate critical
problem areas in which the functioning of government and management on the particular campus might be most clearly studied.
Their interest was not in the specific problem or in a judgment
as to what should or should not be done about it. Inferences from
the data may not legitimately offer conclusions on what to do

Exh

CHECK _____ V

Problem Areas, Pre-IHE ITEM IS A PROBLEM ON YOUR CAMPUS.

If your major area of concern is not included , list it here:

13_____

Which of the boxes represent the areas that you feel
most concerned about on your campus?   Check: _____

1. _____   3. _____   5. _____   7. _____   9. _____   11. _____   13. _____
2. _____   4. _____   6. _____   8. _____   10. _____   12. _____

PE(RESOURCES

Administrators, Fac ace, Equipment, Funds
Trustees

POLICIES AND PROCEDURES

Rules and Regulations (number, establishment,
enforcement, change)

INTELLECTUAL CLIMATE

____Intellectual discussion
____Independent study
____Quality of students
____Quality of faculty
____Quality of administration

ons and

and

for indi-

5.
____Performing facilities for art,
music and drama
____Museum and collections
____Financial support for research
____Financial support for humani-
ties and arts
____Provision for artistic perform-
ances, resident scholars, etc.

Other _____

____Censorship
____Controversial speakers
____Protests and demonstrations
related to social and political
issues
____Academic freedom
____Policy on sponsored research
____Freedom of expression and
practices in the classroom

9.
____Political participation of
faculty
____Opportunity for experimenta-
tion in teaching
____Opportunity to pursue indi-
vidual interests
____Opportunities to initiate
change in this area

Other _____

ACADEMIC PROGRAM

____Teaching methods--discussion,
lecture, experimental techni-
ques
____Teaching ability--presentation,
stimulation
____Academic advising
____Testing methods
____Administrative support for
innovative practices

Other _____

2 e halls

:ilities

6.
____Student study space
____Computer
____Audio-visual equipment and
services
____Bookstore
____Financial support for instruc-
tion

____Grading practices
____Course prerequisites
____Departmental organization
____Requirements for the degree
____Requirements for the major
field
____Procedures for registration

10.
____Opportunity to initiate cur-
ricular reform
____Opportunity to participate
in curricular decisions
____Freedom to initiate new
courses
____Opportunity to review existing
courses

Other _____

STUDENT LIFE

____Informal contacts between stu-
dents, faculty and administration
____Respect of faculty and adminis-
tration for students
____Sense of community
____Responsiveness of faculty
____Responsiveness of administrators

Other _____

3

trans-

7.
____Recreational and sports--
stadium and field
____Intramural sports and facili-
ties
____Informal social space
____Space for meetings and
activities
____Financial support for student
services

____Regulations about drugs
____Regulations about sex
____Regulations about alcohol
____Regulations about dress
____Regulations about gambling
____Regulations about dormitory
hours

11
____Opportunity to participate in
establishing social regulations
____Opportunity to participate in
changing social regulations
____Opportunity to participate in
student government
____Quality of student govern-
ment

Other _____

WORKING CONDITIONS

____Class size
____Time for research, scholarship,
creative work
____Relations between faculty and
administration
____Relations between faculty and
staff
____Stimulation from colleagues

Other _____

4.

e space
d

lerical

8.
____Financial support for staff
and equipment
____Special equipment (tape
recorders, calculators,
pianos)
____Faculty and staff parking and
transportation
____Faculty club

____Class schedules and teaching
loads
____Promotions and tenure
____Salaries and fringe benefits
____Sabbatical leave and attend-
ance at professional meetings
____Hiring and firing
____Opportunity to participate in
departmental decisions

12.
____Opportunity to participate in
institutional decisions
____Opportunity to participate in
faculty governance: committees, senate, etc.
____Administrative procedures
(payroll, purchasing, etc.)
____Handling of complaints

Other _____

about the problems. This limitation is illustrated by our second highlight, which can be seen in the answers on two particular items, one about "regulations on drugs" and another about "censorship and controversial speakers." The item on drug regulations was checked by so few respondents on community college campuses, public four-year campuses, and private college campuses that it fell more than a 0.5 standard deviation below the average rate of checking for problem areas for all 3,278 respondents. This does not mean that drug use was minimal on all three types of campus. On a Southern community college campus the interview findings suggested minimal drug abuse. On a Northern private college campus, the interview follow-up indicated that drug use was considerable, that faculty were either unaware or were for the most part not troubled as long as discretion prevailed and hard drugs were kept out, and that administrators who knew preferred to keep the matter quiet. Other explanations applied to other campuses.

In the area of censorship and controversial speakers, the PIQ returns yielded this surprising find: For faculty, administrators, and department chairmen of private and public four-year colleges and of community colleges, the checking was at more than a 0.5 standard deviation below the mean of problem areas checked. Let us say of an area with this level of checking that it is "not reported as a problem" for governing at that time by these groups. However, the male students on the four-year campuses, public and private, checked the area of censorship and controversial speakers as a problem with a more than 0.5 standard deviation *above the mean*. Female students on the public four-year campuses joined the male students in checking concern about academic freedom, whereas none of the other populations did. One of our consultants was shocked. Whether the shock is justified, however, cannot be known without closer inquiry into the reasons for the checking and nonchecking by different respondents. Even closer inquiry may put the appraisal of the situation into the domain of contestable judgments. On the drug regulation issue, for example, the CGP interviewers' notes reflected their chairman's view that the private campus president who wanted to "keep the lid on" the growing use of drugs on his campus was making a misjudgment. What was, on the questionnaire returns, "not reported as a problem" was precisely for that reason a potentially dangerous governance matter.

HIGHLIGHT 3. WHO CHECKED MOST?

A second type of unwarranted inference from the PIQ data should be noted. The inference that people think that "things are bad" may not be validly made from the fact that they check a problem area with extraordinary frequency.

The PIQ data show, for example, that among public university faculty responding, the humanities faculty checked an average of 52 out of the 120 problem areas (51.96, or 8.66 per set), whereas the engineering faculty checked only 32 on the average. The averages for all academic areas are shown in Table 2.

Table 2. Frequency of responses of public four-year college and university faculty by academic area (Pre-Interview Questionnaire, 1967)

Academic area	Average number of problem areas checked (Total possible: 120)
Humanities	51.96
Social sciences	47.58
Natural sciences	41.28
Education	37.14
Business	35.88
Engineering	31.86

Among students as well as faculty, and in private and community colleges as well as public four-year colleges, the respondents from humanities and social sciences checked more problem areas per person than did those from either education, business, or engineering.

There was also a significant difference in the number of problem areas checked by total respondents from each of the different types of campus (Table 3). This does not mean that the public colleges are in the greatest turmoil, that they are the lowest quality institutions, that their students, faculty, and administrators are the most alienated, or that their problems are the severest or least well handled. Similarly one may not infer from these data that humanities people are most disgruntled, have the worst problems, are the most likely to revolt, or have the poorest programs.

There is an old adage that the squeaky wheel gets the most grease. If money and facilities are the grease of campus, we cannot report that the most frequent checking pointed either to those who were getting the most or those who were neediest. As depicted in the subjective judgments of interviewers and the evidence of budgets, some of the colleges with the best-supported humanities departments and with relatively superior facilities for humanities were nevertheless ones in which humanities people checked more problems than did those in natural sciences and education.

Table 3. Frequency of responses of college and university faculty (Pre-Interview Questionnaire, 1967)

Type of campus by control	Rank in frequency of checking by all on campus
Public four-year college or university	Highest frequency
Private colleges	2nd highest
Community colleges (public)	Lowest frequency

In speculating about these data, it is instructive to seek related findings in other research. In the work of Stern (using the AI and the CCI) and Pace (using a shorter version derived from the CCI and called College and University Environment Scales) it has been found that the frequency of controversy and criticism of a college and its administration is greater on campuses which have relatively more distinguished records in producing graduates who go on to the doctorate, win national fellowships, and the like. Without attributing special merit to this particular type of outcome, one can hypothesize that the different academic areas and types of college tend to be associated with somewhat different intellectual and expressive styles. In his study of responses from 382 campuses about campus unrest, Astin suggested that students were not "verbally aggressive" on protest-prone campuses. He further summarized his findings in these words:

> Apparently institutions which experienced more disruptive and violent protests than would be anticipated from the characteristics of their entering students tended to be universities, coeducational colleges, and public colleges.
> Institutions that had fewer protests than one would expect . . . tended to be four-year colleges, technical

schools, liberal arts colleges, and private non-sectarian
colleges and to have environments characterized by a
high degree of concern for the individual student.

Unrest, at least that of a disruptive or violent
nature, is in part a response to a feeling that the welfare
of the individual student is slighted.

Astin characterized the "protest-prone institutions" as having
"environments which were incohesive; moreover, students and
faculty had little involvement in the class; students were not
on warm, friendly terms with the instructor; and they were not
verbally aggressive. . . ." [4]

The frequency of expressed concern, then, need not be an
unhealthy sign for a campus. Astin's interpretation suggests that
campuses which combine active debate and warm relations with
high expressiveness about problems may be less prone to more
destructive expressions about their difficulties. This idea is related in Chapter 3 to the role of feeling and idea in the processes
of developing consent in campus governance.

A further speculation about the data on frequency of checking is that it may have its greatest importance as a clue to who
is reaching out for involvement and as an indicator of the locus
of felt problems.

HIGHLIGHT 4. HOW PROBLEM AREAS DIFFER
FROM CAMPUS TO CAMPUS

A fourth highlight of the PIQ data emerges in different patterns
of checking on different campuses. That one campus has different
problem areas from another at any given time is hardly news.
Specifically how these differ, however, suggests why an improvement in one place may not work in another. For example, on one
private college campus over 50 percent of the male students
pointed to participation in the determination of degree requirements as a problem area, whereas no faculty, department heads,
or administrators did so. The concern of students might have
been expected to cause at least some faculty and staff to note the
area as a problem, and the lack of such notice on an activist
campus could be seen by outsiders as potentially explosive. On
one of the community college campuses, however, over one-third

---

[4] *College and University Bulletin* 22: 1, 5; October 1, 1969.

of the administrators were concerned about the low degree of student participation in governance, whereas less than 10 percent of students reported such a concern. (Interviews disclosed the direction of concern; questionnaires gave the percentages pointing to the concern.)

It could be argued that somewhere between these two extremes there is a healthful degree and pattern of student participation and staff concern; but it seems most unlikely that, even with a cooling process in one place and a stimulating one in the other, the appropriate mechanisms or type of expected engagement of students should be the same. Both campuses present a need for an effort in communication about governance between staff and students, but the climates and directions of needed effort are quite different.

A convenient way to see the differences among campuses on reported problem areas is provided in Exhibit 2, where two kinds of information are combined: (a) how the constituent groups (faculty, department chairmen, male students, female students, and administrators) differ on the same campus in their frequency of checking of problem areas within a set; and (b) how the patterns of checking by these groups differ from one campus to another. For these graphs to be fully intelligible, explanation is needed for the term "set," for the naming of the sets, and for the way of graphing.

With 3,278 respondents and 120 items, of which the average respondent checked more than 40, the potential combinations of checked items were staggering. To extract some meaningful order from these data a mathematical technique was used which sorts the answers into the smallest number of groupings that can account for the highest proportion of answers. This technique, a form of factor analysis, does not provide the explanation for the groupings. The explanation has to be a set of hypotheses about what characterizes the groupings, once they have emerged from the purely inductive process of asking for which items there is the highest correlation of respondent checking of other items. The first such sorting of the 3,278 PIQ responses gave twenty-nine groups. The Nineteen Campus Study team studied the items making up these groups and gave names to them which seemed to typify what the items had in common within each group. By naming a group and by arranging respondents' checking of items by frequency in such a group, we created a scale. To use twenty-nine scales to summarize data, however, is still very

Exhibit 2

Comparison of Responses of Constituents of Two Public Universities by Role Groups and Sets (Pre-Interview Questionnaire, 1967)

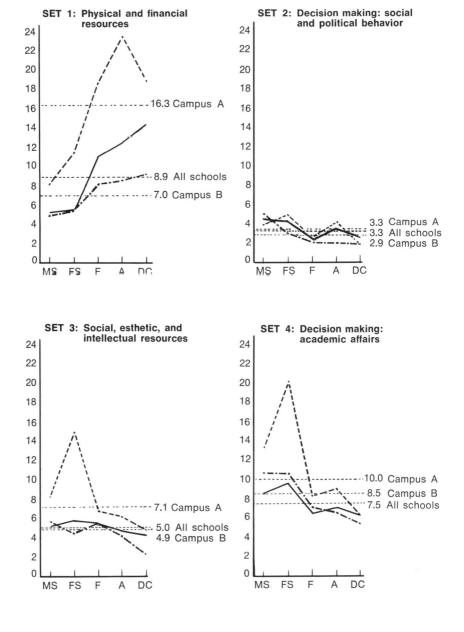

Exhibit 2 (continued)

SET 5: The educational milieu

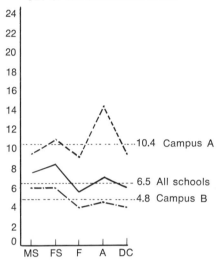

Role groups:

MS Male students
FS Female students
F Faculty
A Administrators
DC Department
chairmen

**SET 6:. Faculty and students
as resources**

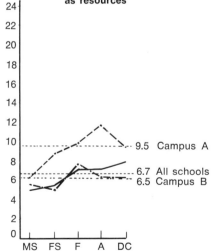

_ _ _ _ Average response
by role group at
campus A.

―――― Average response by
role group at all
schools tested.

._._._. Average response
by role group at
campus B.

.... Mean of all
responses

Exhibit 3

Categories, Sets, and Scales Derived from Responses to the Pre-Interview Questionnaire

Category One: Institutional Resources			Category Two: Interpersonal Processes		
Set 1: Physical & financial resources	**Set 6:** Faculty & students as resources	**Set 3:** Social, es- thetic & intellectual resources	**Set 2:** Decision making: social & political	**Set 5:** Educational milieu	**Set 4:** Decision making: academic affairs
4 Office space	11 Research & publi- cations	23 Athletic facilities	28 Decision making af- fecting	6 Teach- ing	17 Decision making af- fecting
2 Office services	14 Faculty- staff re- lationships	3 Space & resources for student activities	student life	12 Aca- demic re- quire- ments	faculty
27 Finan- cial sup- port for education	13 Intra- faculty relation-	7 Student identifi- cation	5 Regula- tion of student so- cial be-	15 Counsel- ing & ad-	24 Adminis- trative re- sponsiveness to faculty &
25 Teach- ing equip- ment	ships 18 Student & faculty	with the college 8 Resources	havior 22 Parking, transpor-	vising 20 Student dignity	students 29 Trust 10 Decision
1 Research resources	quality 27 Finan-	for the arts	tation & dormi- tories	9 Class load & size	making af- fecting curriculum
26 Language & science labs	cial sup- port for educ. progress	19 Library, bookstore & study space		10 Decision making af- fecting	19 Library, bookstore & study space
22 Parking, transporta- tion & dormitories	7 Student identifi- cation			curriculum 21 Student government	
13 Intra-fac- ulty rela- tionships	with the college				

NOTE: Numbers before each item indicate scale number.

complex. To organize the data still more simply, a second sorting was done to see which of the scales were most highly correlated with others in the respondents' checking. This sorting yielded six second-order groups, which were studied and named, to produce what are here called *sets*. A third sorting located these sets in two *categories*. (For a technical statement on this sorting, see Appendix C.) The two categories, six sets, and twenty-nine scales, as named, are given in Exhibit 3.

In naming the scales, sets, and categories, the researchers abstracted from the original data and, in effect, added an element of speculation and synthesis in a search for their meaning. Some input of the biases and values of the interpreters is unavoidable if anything more than mere tallying and grouping is to be done, but this input marks a point at which other groupings and interpretations might serve better. For example, one staff member sorted the data by campus rather than by the entire 3,278 respondent population. This process yielded somewhat different groupings for each campus, and these groupings naturally suggested somewhat different explanations and names for what was common to them from what are given in the scales and sets for the larger population of respondents. The point of using the larger population is that it permits comparisons among campuses as well as among role groups, age groups, and so on.

The scales and sets, therefore, make it possible to show the graphic differences between campuses which are shown in Exhibit 2. Table 4 shows the differences between Campus A and Campus B, extracted from Exhibit 2. Both are public university campuses, one located in the Midwest, the other in a large Eastern urban setting. Both have enrollments in excess of 10,000. Yet the frequency of checking on Campus A is almost double that of Campus B for the highest set, and four of the six sets on Campus A get a higher rate of checking than the highest on Campus B. In addition, the rank order of concern is utterly different on the two campuses, with general resources first on Campus A and the educational milieu first on Campus B, and with resources for social and esthetic experience second on Campus A but fifth on Campus B.

Even the similarities of response on the two campuses take on a completely different meaning when coupled with the interview findings. The control of social and political behavior, for example, ranked last in frequency of checking on both campuses. Campus A was in turmoil about a political issue at the time of the

interviews, which came only three months after the questionnaire
data were taken, and the issue was active throughout this period.
Campus B, on the other hand, could hardly have been calmer;
whatever issues bestirred it, they were not of a political nature.
One plausible interpretation of the common low ranking of this
set is that each campus' students, faculty, and administrators felt
that its own regulations on social and political behavior were
appropriate. The issues being fought within those regulations,
the degree of disagreement, and the level of emotion expressed,
however, were sharply different.

Table 4. Order of frequency of checking by set, all respondents of two public university campuses (Pre-Interview Questionnaire, 1967)

	Campus A		Campus B	
Set no. and description	Average checks per respondent	Rank in frequency	Average checks per respondent	Rank in frequency
Set 1—Physical and financial resources	16.3	1	7.0	2
Set 2—Decision making: social and political behavior	3.3	6	2.9	6
Set 3—Social, esthetic and intellectual resources	10.4	2	4.8	5
Set 4—Decision making: academic affairs	7.1	5	4.9	4
Set 5—Educational milieu	10.0	3	8.5	1
Set 6—Faculty and students as resources	9.5	4	6.5	3

The points of relevance of these data to the tasks of governance are numerous. One in particular is noteworthy. It has
to do with who can lead effectively and work congenially on
different campuses. The "market" for administrators and faculty
tends today to be a national one, particularly within the domain
of public institutions. Yet an administrator ideally suited to
Campus B could not, in the judgment of our study staff, survive
on Campus A; and an ideal dean or president on Campus A might
succeed well on Campus B but find himself chafed by its priorities
and pace. Similarly, a typical student of Campus A would be

seriously underchallenged on Campus B and unhappy with its
social and political climate, while the student most likely to choose
Campus B would be overwhelmed by the demands of Campus A
and unhappy with its values.

In Chapter 3 the needs of campuses for leaders from their
various constituencies are considered as a crucial factor in their
governance. These data and speculations about who may best
make up different campuses lead to the further speculation that
leadership training for higher education should probably put
greater stress on the fit of leader to context than has been typical. Leaders, according to this speculation, would need to be
trained in the contexts they would serve in (or in similar ones)
or else be trained with special emphasis upon developing the
capacity to adjust to different campus contexts and to analyze
campus and self to recognize when an assignment would be
congenial and effective.

HIGHLIGHT 5. SETS OF PROBLEMS CHECKED MOST

A fifth feature of the PIQ data was the unexpected concentration
of responses upon items related to money and facilities and the
overall checking of resources problems at a higher frequency
than problems of human interactions. One way to measure this
concentration (or, inversely, dispersion) of responses was used
in obtaining the scales and sets; 69 percent of the checking fell
upon the items contributing most heavily to the twenty-nine
scales, and 60 percent of that checking fell into the scales contributing most to the six sets. A measure resulting from this
sorting (shown in Exhibit 18, Appendix C) gives the relationships listed in Table 5. Sets 1, 3, and 6 may be viewed as dealing
with resources problems, with a gradation from the most tangible
(money, facilities) to the least tangible (quality of faculty and
students). Sets 2, 4, and 5 deal with human interactions, with
the social and political ones drawing most frequent attention and
the strictly educational ones the least. This grouping of sets was
the one which emerged in the third-order factoring, with the first
group the heavy contributor to distribution of responses.

In interpreting and speculating upon these relationships,
recall again the danger of trying to link frequency of checking
with either importance or urgency. Since the instructions for
checking problem areas did not call for ranking by importance

or urgency, and since no limit was put upon the number of problem areas to be checked, one might speculate that resources problems got high billing because they were so visible. This "high visibility hypothesis" might be supported by the curious fact that "parking space" repeatedly had a high frequency of checking. Even on private residential college campuses today many students have cars and a number of faculty live at a distance. Commuters to community colleges and large universities add to the list of those who daily encounter the parking problem. Hardly anyone would say that institutional quality is measured by the sufficiency and convenience of parking lots, but more people will converge in noticing their inadequacy than in spotting the difficulties in changing the degree requirements.

Table 5. **Measure of contributions of the six sets of scales to the respondents' total checking (Pre-Interview Questionnaire, 1967)**

	Contribution
Set 1—Physical and financial resources	8.86
Set 2—Decision making: social and political behavior	3.08
Set 3—Social, esthetic and intellectual resources	1.80
Set 4—Decision making: academic affairs	1.42
Set 5—Educational milieu	1.23
Set 6—Faculty and students as resources	1.07

On one campus the administration had been on a drive for a library building and had given the effort great publicity. The need for library facilities obtained a very large number of checks on that campus. Shortly after the questionnaire was administered, the fund-raising goal for the library building was met. The "problem," relative to others in the realm of academic program and educational experience, was not one that had been especially difficult for that college. If frequency of checking were an index of awareness of need, and if high awareness of need could be linked by campus leaders to intensive effort, it might be concluded that campus leaders could cultivate an image of success by highlighting resources problems, but could also in the process divert energy from more significant problems that are more difficult to overcome. At the organizing stage in the 1960's, faculty unions on a number of campuses made parking space one of the issues.

One way to gain political support would be to take credit for getting resources applied to a problem on which tangible gains are easy to show.

A quite different interpretation of these data would be that the best way to grapple with the educational tasks of a campus is to muster the relevant monetary and physical resources. On this basis attention in problem-oriented discussion could be expected to turn to the means with which the people on campus would be able to work out their other problems. If this speculation were sound, the high concentration of administrator and department chairman responses upon resource issues would reflect competent judgment on their part as to where the campus' needs might best be tackled. On this notion, the radicals who score ideological points in debate but are unconcerned about getting control of resources and facilities would be no threat; but the faculty who show more frequent concern with budgets would be the ones likely to wrest power from its previous holders.

A third speculation would link checking of problems with immediate self-interest. This basis for checking problems is not the same as either visibility or perceived effectiveness as points to take hold of problems. Data bearing upon the self-interest hypothesis were obtained by studying the reported degree of sharing of concerns by different role groups; these data yielded the sixth highlight.

HIGHLIGHT 6: WHO IS MOST CONCERNED ABOUT WHAT?

A sixth highlight of the PIQ data has to do with the degree to which faculty, students, administrators, and department chairmen do or do not share in checking the same problem areas. To study the question as to who most often reports concern about what problem areas, we began with the responses from public four-year colleges and universities. Each role group's responses were divided into three lists: (a) items of "low reported concern," that is, checked with a frequency lower than the mean for that group's checking on all items, and lower by more than 0.5 of a standard deviation; (b) items of "average reported concern," that is, within a 0.5 standard deviation in either direction from that mean; and (c) items of "high reported concern," that is, more than a 0.5 standard deviation above that mean. This test of divergence of checking from the mean for the role group was used to locate the most striking differences among groups, because the number of differences meeting the test of statistical significance at the 0.01 level was very large. If one role group—male students, for example—showed "high reported concern" on the same item as another group—faculty, for example—it is "shared as a high frequency concern." The possible combinations of sharing degrees of concern between two groups are thus:

Shared high

Shared average

Shared low

Low concern in one group, high in the other

Average concern in one group, high or low in the other

All of these possibilities were exemplified in the responses. On some items, all groups showed high concern; on other items, no group showed high concern. On most items the percentage of checking differs substantially between two or more groups, in varying combinations. Thirteen items, for example, were generally shared as a high reported concern of all five groups—male students, female students, faculty, department chairmen, and administrators (Table 6).

Table 6. Shared high-frequency concerns on public campuses (Pre-Interview Questionnaire, 1967)

Physical and financial resources

    Item 71—Faculty office space

    Item 51—Classroom and lecture space

    Item 45—Space and equipment

    Item 65—Student parking

Decision making: social and political behavior

    Item 83—Protests and demonstrations

Social, esthetic, and intellectual resources

    Item 23—Sense of community

    Item 53—Library holdings

    Item 56—Student study space

The Educational milieu

    Item 13—Academic advising

    Item 21—Informal contacts

    Item 111—Class schedules and teaching load

    Item 31—Class size

    Item 32—Time for research, scholarship, and creative work

---

For nine of these thirteen items, all five groups checked high; for the other four, four of the five groups checked high.

At the other extreme, there were twenty-three items that were generally checked with low frequency: fourteen items checked low by all five groups, another nine by four of the five groups (Table 7).

Since there was no restriction on the number of items a respondent might check, the low checking on items just listed did

Table 7. Shared low-frequency concerns on public campuses (Pre-Interview Questionnaire, 1967)

Physical and financial resources
    Item 55—Language teaching space

Decision making: social and political behavior
    Item 108—Changing social regulations
    Item 107—Establishing social regulations
    Item 102—Regulations about sex
    Item 101—Regulations about drugs
    Item 105—Regulations about gambling
    Item 104—Regulations about dress
    Item 106—Regulations about dormitory hours
    Item 87—Political participation of faculty
    Item 43—Underground publications and films

Social, esthetic, and intellectual resources
    Item 66—Recreation and sports: stadium and fields
    Item 67—Intramural sports and facilities
    Item 38—Commitment to college

Decision making: academic affairs
    Item 118—Opportunity to participate in faculty governance
    Item 116—Opportunity to participate in departmental decisions
    Item 28—Maintenance of confidentiality

The educational milieu
    Item 109—Opportunity to participate in student government

Faculty and students as resources
    Item 85—Policy on sponsored research
    Item 26—Responsiveness of staff
    Item 34—Relations between faculty and staff
    Item 20—Faculty loyalty to their academic field
    Item 40—Role of "Young Turks"
    Item 35—Stimulation from colleagues

not result from a forced choice of a few high priority concerns. A respondent might also check an item as a problem area not because he felt dissatisfied with what was being done about it, but because he sensed that enough others were dissatisfied to make it a legitimate subject of concern.

Twenty-eight items were of high frequency concern to only two or three of the five groups. Of these items, eight were of high concern to male and female students only (Table 8).

Table 8. Shared concerns, high-frequency, male and female students only, on public campuses (Pre-Interview Questionnaire, 1967)

Social, esthetic, and intellectual resources
>   Item   30—School spirit
>   Item   59—Bookstore

Decision making: academic affairs
>   Item 100—Opportunity to review existing courses

The educational milieu
>   Item   11—Teaching methods
>   Item   12—Teaching ability
>   Item   14—Testing methods
>   Item   91—Grading practices
>   Item   62—Health and counseling services

The last six items prompt the speculation that students are dissatisfied with faculty services (high checking does not always imply dissatisfaction). Failure of faculty and administrators to check these items as much might be caused by their having more realistic expectations, by oversight, or by self-interest. The fact that faculty do show highly frequent concern for Item 9—Commitment to Teaching suggests a basis for student dissatisfaction.

Eight items were checked with high frequency by faculty, administrators, and department chairmen only. They all have to do directly with servicing and compensating the faculty (Table 9).

Eleven other items were of high concern to two or three groups, but in combinations other than those listed above; e.g., male students, faculty, and administrators could converge on an item, or female students, department chairmen, and faculty on another.

A number of items were of high concern to only one role group. Of these seven "belonged" to male students, four to female

Table 9. Shared concerns, high-frequency, for faculty, administrators, and department chairmen only, on public campuses (Pre-Interview Questionnaire, 1967)

Physical and financial resources
  Item 76—Secretarial and/or clerical services
  Item 60—Financial support for instruction
  Item 114—Sabbatical leave and attendance at professional meetings
  Item 113—Salaries and fringe benefits
  Item 48—Financial support for research
  Item 77—Financial support for staff and equipment
  Item 79—Faculty and staff parking and transportation

Decision making: academic affairs
  Item 80—Faculty club

Table 10. Concerns checked with high frequency by only one role group on public campuses (Pre-Interview Questionnaire, 1967)

Set and Item	Role group*				
	MS	FS	F	A	DC
Decision making: social and political					
103—Regulations about alcohol	X				
81—Censorship	X				
Social, esthetic, and intellectual resources					
64—Student union	X				
49—Financial support for humanities and arts				X	
Decision making: academic affairs					
120—Handling of complaints	X				
25—Responsiveness of administrators	X				
97—Opportunities to initiate change in academic area		X			
112—Promotions and tenure			X		
5—Quality of administration			X		
33—Relations between faculty and administration			X		
The educational milieu					
1—Intellectual discussion		X			
22—Respect of faculty and administration for students	X				
7—Liberal vs. professional education					X
16—Interest in courses		X			
27—Availability of counseling		X			
9—Commitment to teaching			X		
Faculty and students as resources					
4—Quality of faculty		X			

* MS = Male students   A = Administrators
  FS = Female students   DC = Department chairmen
  F = Faculty

students, four to faculty, one to administrators, and one to department chairmen (Table 10).

On the total 120 items, there was an older generation vs. younger generation "split" on the 9 items listed high by the elders, 8 by male and female students, and 11 by either male or female students but not their elders. On 36 items (30 percent of the total) virtually all constituencies agreed in checking high or low. For these campuses, then, there is hardly a case for treating the generation gap as fundamental.

A modification on the speculation about self-interest in checking is that people particularly check the items which affect their interests, but which they cannot themselves control. A further suggestion, accounting for both the high emphasis upon resource problems and for nonagreement among role groups on other items, is that the less tangible problems are harder to state in terms that gain wide recognition, so any given list is likely to get less frequent checking of the intangibles than would a list of similar length about tangible needs.

The interests natural to the different roles would seem to account better than other hypotheses for both congruence and disparity of responses. For example, both students and faculty checked high on "faculty office space" and "classroom space" because their roles normally occasion their meeting in these places. Parietal regulations, however, get much less checking from public college faculty than from their students. Administrators outrank all others in the predominance of their checking of resources items. One way to test the relation of role to choice of problems is obtained by comparing the faculty's ordering of

---

Table 11. Comparative order of checking by faculty and total respondents, by sets, public campuses (Pre-Interview Questionnaire, 1967)

Set	Order of overall frequency	Order of faculty frequency
Physical and financial resources	1st	1st
Decision making: social and political	2nd	6th
Social, esthetic, and intellectual resources	3rd	5th
Decision making: academic affairs	4th	4th
The educational milieu	5th	3rd
Faculty and students as resources	6th	2nd

Table 12. Rank order of concern on campus problems,
comparison by role groups, axis A (Pre-Interview
Questionnaire, 1967)

Group of problem areas	Faculty order	Administrator order
Resources problems	3rd	1st
People's interactions	2nd	2nd
Policies and procedures	1st	3rd

sets of items (from most frequently checked downward) with that for all respondents. Findings based on the data for public colleges (to screen out the significant effect of type of campus control) are shown in Table 11.

This order remains when faculty responses are grouped by their academic area, with two exceptions: Education faculty put problems of the educational milieu above those of faculty and students as resources. Natural sciences faculty put problems of social, esthetic, and intellectual resources above those of decision making in academic affairs. These variations might be explained, on these campuses, by a special professional interest of education faculty and a common disinterest of natural scientists in the issues of regulating academic affairs.

The relevance of role to perception of problems is even more strikingly seen in another kind of data obtained on the Pre-Interview Questionnaire. Respondents were asked to select that one of the twelve "boxes" of problem areas (see Exhibit 1) which most concerned them, and to nominate people with information and influence in that area. (These "boxes of problems" are not the same as the factors obtained by factor analysis and providing the basis for the six sets.) The problem areas were presented on two axes. Axis A divided problems into those of resources, interactions of people, and policies and procedures. On this dimension the order of priority of concern was quite different for faculty and administrators (Table 12).

Students divided choices fairly even among three groups. Axis B classified problems as those of working conditions, intellectual climate, academic program, and student life. Data on this breakdown yielded a different contrast among student, faculty, and administrator choices of prime concern; this time administrators spread their concerns fairly even among the four groups, while students and faculty diverged (Table 13).

The performance of the roles of faculty, students, department chairmen, and administrators is, of course, central to the functioning of a campus. These data confirm the commonsense recognition that the roles are associated with different perceptions of problems. The different perceptions have various causes from self-interest to opportunity for influence to opportunity to observe. Effective functioning of a campus involves the development of ways for all of these perceptions to be taken into full account.

Table 13. Rank order of concern on campus problems, comparison by role groups, axis B (Pre-Interview Questionnaire, 1967)

Group of problem areas	Faculty order	Student order
Working conditions	1st	4th
Intellectual climate	2nd	3rd
Academic program	3rd	2nd
Student life	4th	1st

This judgment is not implied by these data. It is a matter of hypothesis or speculation. The judgment itself does not imply a specific approach to dealing with the different perceptions, such as membership on councils and committees for students and faculty. In Chapter 3 doubts will be raised about concentration upon any one approach to this task. Different approaches, however, could well reflect specific attention to these campus roles as a feature of campus governance.

Further speculation about these data has to do with polarization on campuses. The cited differences and likenesses of problem checking by role groups form a very complex pattern for the nineteen campuses studied here. These data in themselves can hardly be said to give a picture of polarization.

Why then did two of the nineteen campuses erupt into violent confrontation within months after our data were taken? In one of the confrontations some students and faculty initially pressed a sympathetic administration for more than it believed right and more than it was permitted to grant by the controlling regents and legislature. Compared with the range of issues here surveyed, the ones in the focus of that controversy were quite few. The determination of the petitioners, on the one hand, and the limits

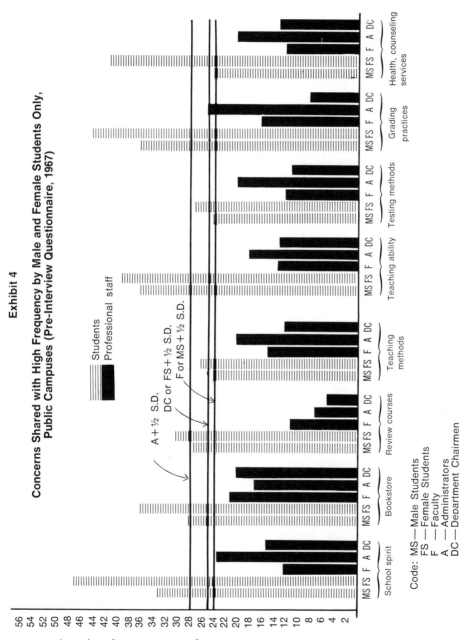

Exhibit 4

Concerns Shared with High Frequency by Male and Female Students Only, Public Campuses (Pre-Interview Questionnaire, 1967)

Students

Professional staff

(Measured in percentage of constituency response)

Code: MS — Male Students
FS — Female Students
F — Faculty
A — Administrators
DC — Department Chairmen

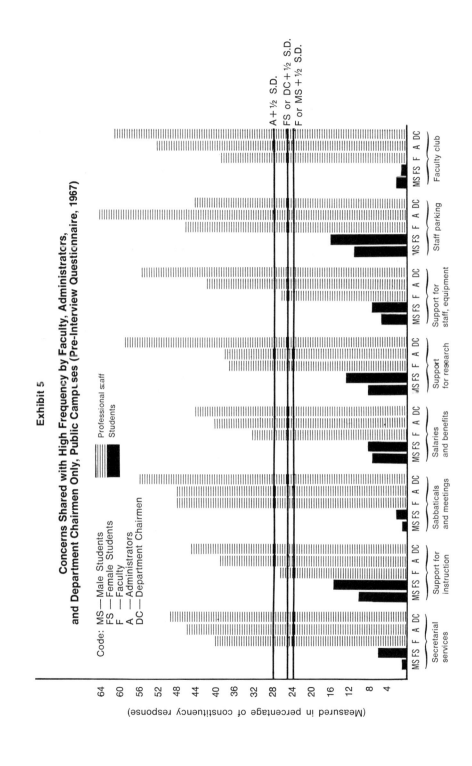

Exhibit 5

Concerns Shared with High Frequency by Faculty, Administrators, and Department Chairmen Only, Public Campuses (Pre-Interview Questionnaire, 1967)

Code: MS —Male Students
FS —Female Students
F —Faculty
A —Administrators
DC—Department Chairmen

Professional staff
Students

(Measured in percentage of constituency response)

Exhibit 6

Concerns Shared with High Frequency by Male Students, Public Campuses (Pre-Interview Questionnaire, 1967)

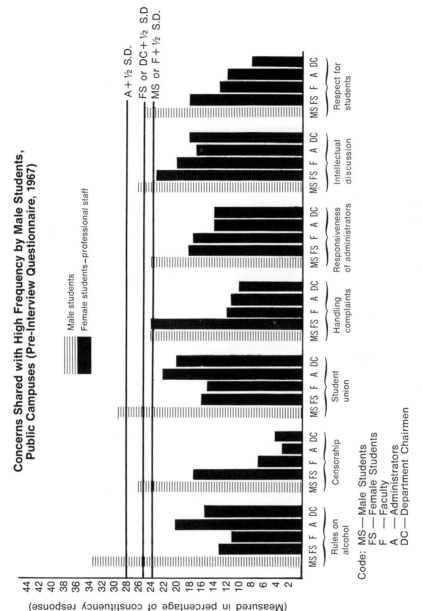

Male students

Female students—professional staff

A + ½ S.D.

FS or DC + ½ S.D

MS or F + ½ S.D.

Respect for students

Intellectual discussion

Responsiveness of administrators

Handling complaints

Student union

Censorship

Rules on alcohol

MS FS F A DC

(Measured in percentage of constituency response)

44 42 40 38 36 34 32 30 28 26 24 22 20 18 16 14 12 10 8 6 4 2

Code: MS — Male Students
FS — Female Students
F — Faculty
A — Administrators
DC — Department Chairmen

Exhibit 7

Concerns Shared with High Frequency by Female Students, Public Campuses (Pre-Interview Questionnaire, 1967)

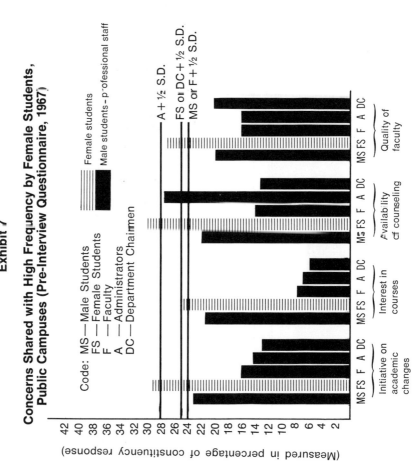

Exhibit 8

Concerns Shared with High Frequency by Faculty Only, Public Campuses (Pre-Interview Questionnaire, 1967)

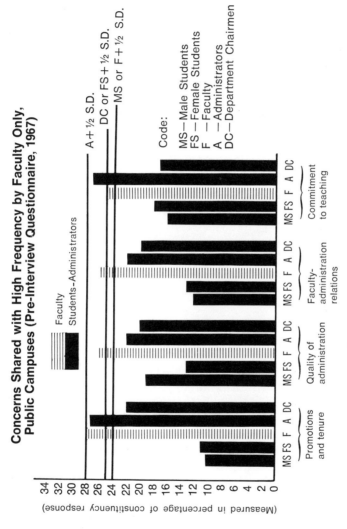

Legend:
- Faculty
- Students–Administrators

Reference lines:
- A + ½ S.D.
- DC or FS + ½ S.D.
- MS or F + ½ S.D.

Code:
- MS — Male Students
- FS — Female Students
- F — Faculty
- A — Administrators
- DC — Department Chairmen

Y-axis (vertical): 34 32 30 28 26 24 22 20 18 16 14 12 10 8 6 4 2 0

(Measured in percentage of constituency response)

Categories (X-axis): Promotions and tenure (MS FS F A DC); Quality of administration (MS FS F A DC); Faculty-administration relations (MS FS F A DC); Commitment to teaching (MS FS F A DC) imposed from the outside by the regents and legislature, on the other hand, brought the issues to violence. The president resigned, and the regents chose a man who would do their will. In the other case the source of confrontation was initially a narrow issue about the location, functions, and the process of locating one building. This initial issue was settled, with little violence, after a short period of demonstrations and negotiations. Later, however, conflict moved toward a demand for transformation of the university from a relatively selective public college to an open admissions college. As this thrust moved toward approval, there was a substantial turnover in administration.

Polarization in the forms illustrated by these two cases, then, does not necessarily involve widespread division between role groups on a campus. In these cases it was a minority even within the initiating constituencies who sought their will at the risk of confrontation. The depth of feeling on each side was more critical than the numbers sharing the feeling. The mode of dealing with the feelings seemed to affect substantially the degree of violence experienced and the type of change that resulted. The place of feelings and ideas in governance will be addressed more fully in Chapter 3. That chapter also deals with the possible need for more varied methods of communicating and responding among role groups than are now common.

HIGHLIGHT 7. HOW FACULTY DIFFER AMONG THEMSELVES IN REPORTING PROBLEMS[5]

On the nineteen campuses studied, 1,214 faculty responded to the Pre-Interview Questionnaire. Exhibits 9, 10, and 11 depict the similarities and differences of responses found when they were compared by academic area, age groups, type of campus control, and rank.

On one of the six sets, decision making in academic affairs, the youngest and the next youngest age groups (up to 35, 36-45) checked significantly more problem areas than did the oldest group (46 and up).

On all of the other five sets, the faculty of public colleges listed substantially more problems than did those of private colleges, and those of private colleges more than those of community colleges. The frequency of responses did not vary sig-

---

[5] The study yielding this highlight was done by Stephen Plumer.

Exhibit 9

Faculty Responses to the PIQ by Age Group and Type of Campus

X axis = Age groups
Y axis = Mean number of items checked per respondent

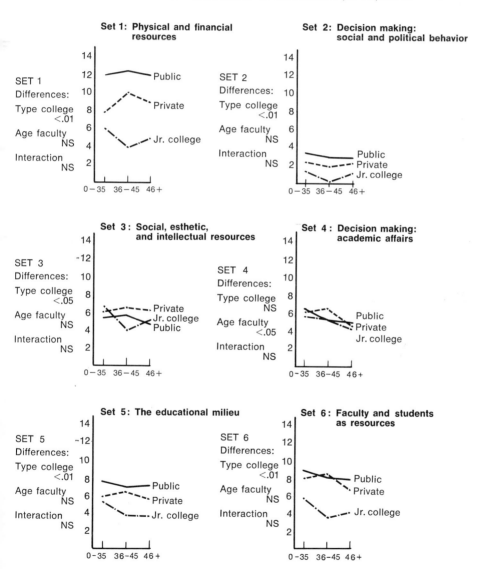

Exhibit 10

Faculty Responses to the PIQ by Rank and Type of Campus

Y Axis: mean number of responses per respondent

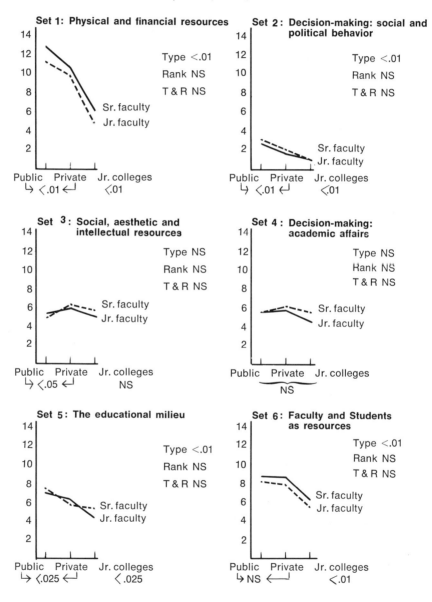

Exhibit 11

Faculty Responses to the PIQ by Type of Campus and Academic Area of Faculty

Y Axis: mean number of responses per respondent
X Axis: academic areas—
  Ad: administrative studies
  Educ: college of education

Tech: college of technical studies
  (e.g., engineering)
Hum: humanities area
S: natural sciences area
SS: social sciences area

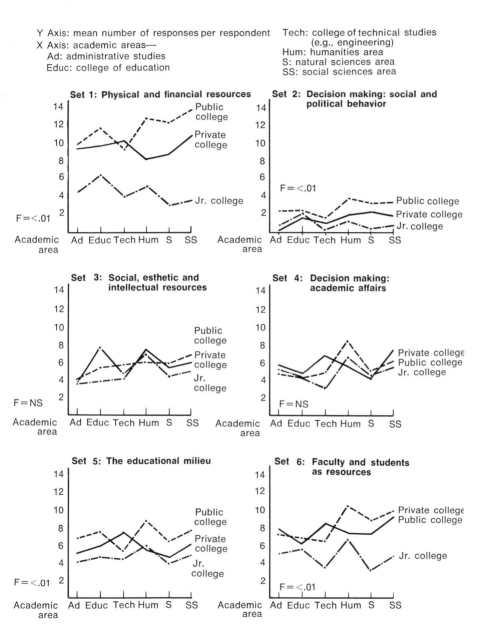

nificantly with rank on any of the sets of items. As noted on page 52, the response rate did vary sharply by academic area when aggregated on all items, with the faculty of humanities, social sciences, and natural sciences checking more problems than did those of education, business, and engineering.

When the more detailed analysis shown in Exhibit 11 was made, with sets of items separated and type of campus control taken into account, a more complex picture appeared. For example, the social scientists of public and private colleges checked physical and financial resources problems somewhat more frequently than did the humanities faculty. In comparison with their colleagues in other areas, the education faculty of community colleges checked relatively more problems of physical and financial resources and of social, esthetic, and intellectual resources than they did on other sets.

There was one domain of problems in which faculty seemed alike on all types of campus; namely, that of problems of decision making in academic affairs. This may also be the area in which the insistence of faculty upon effective voice in governance will be strongest.

HIGHLIGHT 8. HOW PRIVATE, PUBLIC, AND COMMUNITY COLLEGES DIFFER IN PROBLEMS REPORTED[6]

Reference has already been made to the fact that public four-year campuses reported problems with the greatest frequency, and community colleges with the least. Size, complexity, and intellectual climate (as in the contrast in Exhibit 2 between Campuses A and B, both public) may have more to do with this ordering than disaffection or severity of problems. While intellectual climate may correlate in some degree with selectivity and academic prestige, it cannot be taken as a specific measure of the quality of performance of an institution's task. In fact, if it is the purpose of a particular private or public college to employ "open admissions," it would be dysfunctional for it to emulate the curriculum of a selective college, and it seems unlikely that similar forms of governance or management would serve the two types of college equally well.

---

[6] The study here reported was done by Suzanne Imes under the direction of Stephen Plumer and Michael Metty.

Community colleges in the sample were larger than the private four-year colleges, and they were less complex in curriculum and organization than the public four-year institutions and some of the private colleges. In the data cited in Highlight 4 the point is also illustrated that student interest in governance was much higher in some of the private colleges than in some of the community colleges.

Although the frequency of checking of problems by faculty of public, private, and community colleges differed sharply in amount (as seen in Exhibits 9—11), the directions of concern were generally parallel between public and private college faculty: physical and financial resources were of the most frequent concern, with faculty and students as resources next; least checking was given for decision making on social and political behavior. Public college faculty gave third most checks to problems of social, esthetic, and intellectual resources; whereas private college faculty gave third and a close fourth place to the educational milieu and problems of academic decision making. The community college faculty, like the others, put problems of decision making on social and political behavior in last place but gave almost equal checking to all of the other five sets. Insofar as they put any sets of problems in the forefront, it was not problems of physical and financial resources or faculty and students as resources, but problems of decision making in academic affairs and social, esthetic, and intellectual resources.

Speculation on the specific meaning of these differences is hazardous, but the high ranking of problems of decision making in academic affairs in community colleges is of interest. The five community college campuses studied were not "hot spots" of faculty–administration tension; quite the contrary. Yet a number of other studies have pointed to the community college heritage of secondary school attitudes toward faculty, and the relatively undeveloped patterns of professionalism among faculty in these institutions. Our data probably reflect traces of this background.

Student responses also reflected some differences between community colleges, on the one hand, and the four-year colleges and universities, on the other hand. For example, issues of control of social and political behavior were more often reported by public and private college students than by other groups. On the control of the academic program (set 4) the most concerned people were public and private college students. Their reporting concentrated on ten of the fourteen items on this subject, particularly on six dealing with curricular and institutional change. This area of concern was less in evidence among community college students. On items about the educational milieu (set 5) a less marked, but parallel, difference existed. On the seven items related to teaching, students checked more frequently than faculty and administrators on all types of campuses. However, on the four items about academic requirements, on four items on counseling and advising, and on items related to student dignity, the students at private and public colleges showed more frequent concern than did those at community colleges. These data do not indicate that conditions in these problem areas were worse on the public and private college campuses than the community colleges; they merely reflect a less prevalent expression of concern at the community colleges. This fact itself may call for steps in communications and governance that differ among the campuses. For purposes of governing and managing, lack of expressed concern may be as great a problem as its opposite.

It would be a mistake to convey the impression that the PIQ data present only contrasts between private, public, and community colleges. When all responses from each type of campus were pooled, the areas of predominant concern were in the same order for all three: first, physical and financial resources; second, control of political and social behavior; and third, resources for social, esthetic, and intellectual experience; and so on through the sixth and last, faculty and students as resources. Even to minute particulars there were commonalities; for example, among the problems of space and resources for student activities the food service had greatest notoriety on all types of campus. On some items similarity was greater between private and community colleges than among the four-year institutions; e.g., protests and demonstrations were most checked by all role groups of the public four-year colleges, while items on recreational space were significantly reported only for community and private colleges. Similarly, the five items dealing with resources for the humanities were shared concerns at private and community colleges but had scattered response at public colleges. Only at community colleges was the checking of library and bookstore as resources at a level of more than a 0.5 standard deviation below the mean for all items; yet the library and bookstore resources were far larger and more diverse at public four-year and private campuses.

Two quite different interpretations of this last finding are possible. One is that community college resources, though small and relatively focused, fit their purpose more closely than do those of the other colleges which pursue more complex and more advanced studies. Another possibility is that the fit of resources to task is no better at community colleges than at others, but that a part of the community college prolem is the satisfaction of its participants with what they have. Similarly, though only the junior college respondents frequently checked the quality of students as a problem area, this does not imply that the intake of students should be selective; it may be that the methods and resources for serving them ought to be changed to serve the clientele better.

In view of the differences in purpose, control, size, and clientele among the three types of campuses, the bearings of the PIQ data upon the choice of ways to govern and manage are complex. Representative councils and committees, for example, would be differently received and would have different effectiveness among these differing campuses. A tailoring of governing structures and processes to each campus' conditions would surely be more appropriate to effective performance of its task than would the adoption of a standard approach to the governing of all private or all community or all four-year public colleges.

HIGHLIGHT 9. WHO IS SEEN AS INFORMED OR INFLUENTIAL? [7]

The Pre-Interview Questionnaire was designed, as the name suggests, to obtain data useful in guiding the work of interviewers on the nineteen campuses studied. In addition to checking problem areas, respondents were asked to name persons (by name or title or task) to whom they would go to obtain information and to get something done in the problem area of the respondents' greatest concern. Three spaces were provided for nominees for each of the two questions. The original purpose of these questions was simply to identify persons whom the interviewers should see. The answers, however, when tallied and analyzed, provided other significant information. Shown on pages 69 and 70, for example, is the distribution of nominations by problem area of primary concern. This disclosed differences in primary area of interest among students, faculty, and administrators. Other highlights emerged on these questions: What percentage of the three nomi-

---

[7] The study yielding this highlight was done by Ruth Churchill.

nations of informed persons and influential persons did respondents use? To what extent were the nominations concentrated upon particular individuals and positions? Do these response patterns differ on campuses of different types of control? Do they differ between students, faculty, and administrators? Do they differ between getting information and getting something done?

Since respondents were asked to check only one problem area of primary concern and only three nominees for that area, and since they did not need to know name or exact title for the nominees, a high nomination rate was expected. The rate of checking of problem areas had been quite high, but in contrast, the nomination rate on informed and influential persons was quite low (Table 14).

Table 14. Percentage of nominations of informed and influential people to possible nominations (3 per respondent) (Pre-Interview Questionnaire, 1967)*

	Overall medians	
	For obtaining information	For getting something done
Student respondents	27%	20%
Faculty respondents	37%	27%
Administrator respondents	41%	32%

* See also Exhibit 13.

Several causes for the low rates and for the differences among them were encountered in subsequent interviewing. Simple ignorance as to where to go was one factor. On this score, administrators knew most, and students were most likely to know least. On one campus student nominations on obtaining information were at a 9 percent rate as against 38 percent for faculty; on another the rates were 12 percent for students and 40 percent for administrators. Size and type of campus may be assumed to affect the "awareness" of who has information and can get action. Thus the data show that private college students used a far larger percentage of possible nominations than did other students, with public college students slightly ahead of community college students.

A second reason for nominating one or two rather than three persons was the perception by the respondent that one or two were sufficient, that the desired information was all obtainable, or the influence was concentrated in this person or position. On some campuses more types of information were treated as privileged than on others, and some campuses more than others vigorously pressed important information upon the consciousness of constituents. Also the style of the president and others in delegating authority affected the perception of concentration of influence. (Data on the concentration of nominations upon particular persons and positions are given below.) Among junior college students the nominations on obtaining information varied from 9 percent to 41 percent, and on getting something done from 6 percent to 26 percent. Awareness of who knows and acts may have combined with perception of concentration of knowledge and power to produce these differences.

A third cause for the low rate of nominations was that the desired information or action simply could not be obtained. For example, on a campus not in the study where the PIQ was used and followed by interviews, a new president had done away with his predecessor's "kitchen cabinet," made up of a few insiders who knew things and could get action. The new president would not act upon requests brought directly to him, since he had delegated the authority for acting. But he had also reversed some of the major administrators' most important decisions because he thought them ill conceived. The result was a widespread perception that "nobody knows where to go" and "there's no way to get action on your concern."

The generally lower rate of nominations for getting things done than for obtaining information might be explained by the perception that one person can know all the relevant facts on an issue, but no one can get the needed action by himself. There were campuses, however, where the powers attributed to the president or to a particular dean or vice-president far outreached what he could actually do. On a number of campuses, in fact, the president felt that an exaggerated impression of what he could get done was a key cause of the degree of hostility and the difficulties in getting rational discussion of governance problems.

Though private college respondents generally nominated at a higher rate than others, there were exceptions. The administrators at one public college used over 70 percent of the options to nominate, higher than at any private college. This same college had the lowest rate of all public and private colleges (8 percent) of student nominations on influence. Speculation offered quite divergent explanations: perhaps authority was widely delegated in a way known to administrators but not to students; perhaps, on the contrary, students knew about the table of organization but disbelieved it.

Another public institution had almost the opposite pattern of nominations on getting action: the highest student rate for public campuses (23 percent) and the lowest administrator rate (10 percent). Explanatory hypotheses again diverged: perhaps a good team of administrators was at work and things could get done by initiative with any one of them, as students correctly perceived; but administrators deal with only the chief of the relevant area. Alternatively, the students may have misperceived the situation, while the administrators knew that only a few could get results. In trying to assess the coping and governing strategies of a campus, interviewers were obliged to seek the specific meaning of these different perceptions of the loci of information and influence.

Another perspective on informed and influential persons on campus was obtained by asking: Are the nominations of such persons concentrated upon a few individuals or roles (e.g., academic vice-president)? Data on this question were obtained in the Nineteen Campus Study in two forms: (a) the percentage of nominations given to the single highest nominee, and (b) the smallest number of nominees on a campus necessary to add up to 50 percent of the nominations. On both of these measures, small colleges were distinctly more centralized in nominations than were large colleges (Table 15).

Within the means of the second part of this chart, there are great variations from institution to institution. In one private college the nominations by administrators on getting something done go more than 50 percent to a single position, while the student nominations go to eight different positions before reaching 50 percent. At the same college, the nominations on getting information concentrate on a range from two (by administrators) to nine (by faculty) before 50 percent of the nominations are reached. In one large public institution the faculty nominations on getting information spread over thirty persons before accumulating to 50 percent and over eleven on getting something done, whereas the corresponding nominations by administrators were only seven and four. Junior college nominations tended to mount to 50 percent with only two to four nominations (with three exceptions

n obtaining infor-
control of campus
tralization yielded
the public institu-
reatest dispersion
tions given to one
that junior college
han did other stu-
ns (or positions)
nations, the junior
d private colleges,
ations for getting
nething other than

of nominations of
grouped by size of
Pre-Interview Ques-

A. Percentage of nominations for this area obtained by the highest nominee.

Median scores for—

	Obtaining information			Getting something done		
	Student choice	Faculty choice	Adminst. choice	Student choice	Faculty choice	Adminst. choice
Small colleges	22%	21%	26%	30%	28%	35%
Large colleges	15%	12%	16%	22%	18%	31%

B. Smallest number of nominees required to accumulate to 50% of nominations for area

Median scores for—

	Obtaining information			Getting something done		
	Student choice	Faculty choice	Adminst. choice	Student choice	Faculty choice	Adminst. choice
Small colleges	4.3	3.9	3.0	3.1	2.7	2.4
Large colleges	9.6	11.2	4.2	5.3	5.9	3.0

size is at work as a factor making for the centralization of nominations (Table 16).

Throughout these data administrators concentrated their nominations more heavily than faculty or students. Also, the nominations on getting information were less concentrated than were those on getting something done.

How are these relationships to be explained, and how do they bear upon the problems of governing and managing a campus? Only speculation and hypothesis can be offered on these questions. On small campuses, a smaller number of administrators and faculty are employed and thus are in a position to know and to act than on larger campuses, and those few are more likely to be visible and known. The effect may be one of pin-

---

Table 16. Concentration of nominations, grouped by type of campus control and by role of nominators (Pre-Interview Questionnaire, 1967)

A. Percentage of nominations for his area obtained by the highest nominee

| | Median scores for— | | | | | |
| | Obtaining information | | | Getting something done | | |
	Student choice	Faculty choice	Adminst. choice	Student choice	Faculty choice	Adminst. choice
Community colleges	27%	20%	25%	33%	24%	33%
Private colleges	19%	22%	26%	22%	27%	46%
Public colleges and universities	12%	12%	15%	19%	16%	24%

B. Smallest number of nominees required to accumulate to 50% of nominations for area

| | Mean scores for— | | | | | |
| | Obtaining information | | | Getting something done | | |
	Student choice	Faculty choice	Adminst. choice	Student choice	Faculty choice	Adminst. choice
Community colleges	4.2	3.8	2.8	3.0	3.0	2.8
Private colleges	4.6	4.9	3.1	3.9	2.7	1.9
Public colleges and universities	10.9	12.4	4.6	5.3	6.6	3.4

pointing responsibility and capability to act. This effect could in turn bear upon the finding in other studies that size of campus correlates with frequency of unrest and disruption. (A similar phenomenon is documented for schools by Barker and Gump.[8]) A small campus also typically has a lower number of students per faculty or administrator, with the result that access to the informed and influential people is likley to be easier than on large campuses. Access does not guarantee responsiveness by the influential person, nor understanding by the person who receives the information, nor cooperation, but it does offer at least some hope for these results.

The finding that community colleges reported more centralized nominations than smaller private colleges probably reflects the fact that the community colleges are, for their size, more centralized and less complex organizations. Community colleges are generally less prone to unrest and disruption than four-year colleges, in spite of their size. A number of factors may be assumed to contribute to the willingness of community college students to accept the purposes and priorities of the institutions' leadership, as well as their performance: the social class origins of the students, the type of education being sought by students and supplied by the college (and the relative fit between the two), the proportion of students living at home and having little time for participation in extra-class activities, and the intellectual style and climate.

The dispersion of nominations on large public campuses may also be related to characteristics reported in other studies: their size, complexity, the large degree of decentralization on some matters (e.g., control of curriculum by colleges and departments) and centralization on others (e.g., aggregate financial resources), and the intellectual climates of different campuses.

The effects of the perceived concentration of campus leadership (informed and influential people) may be assumed to differ sharply between the two types of situation: one in which the role groups are relatively united in purpose and priorities, and one in which they are not. In the former case the concentration of leadership could be expected to facilitate achievement and constituent satisfaction if the consensus continues and the circumstances and tasks of the campus do not change substantially. On the campus with divided loyalties, however, a leadership con-

---

[8] *Big School, Small School.* Palo Alto: Stanford University, 1969.

centrated tightly and largely among administrators seems likely to be highly vulnerable. On the defensive, it has poor lines of communications and limited forces. On the offensive, mustering energy for a concerted effort toward its goals, it faces challenges to its credibility among the divided constituents and often inadequate resources to enlist their understanding and collaboration. In Chapter 3 attention is directed to some of the consequent problems of communication and leadership. Since the data earlier reported on role groups indicate a very complex variety of perspectives and priorities among them, campuses would seem well advised to reexamine their policies and mechanisms for enlisting constituency consent if they are to have achievable aims and the leaders are to have a manageable task.

HIGHLIGHT 10. CAMPUS ENVIRONMENTS AND REPORTED PROBLEMS[9]

As the Nineteen Campus Study was being planned, the staff hypothesized that the type and frequency of problems reported might bear a significant relationship to the intellectual climate of the campuses. Different combinations of problems reported and of intellectual climate would, on this hypothesis, call for different priorities in governing and managing and would require different styles and strategies for dealing with those priorities. The staff assumed that if such relationships existed, they would lie close to the heart of currently critical issues of campus governance. It would, however, be extremely difficult to document these connections. The most to be hoped for would be some promising leads. A few such leads did emerge from studies correlating problems reported on the PIQ with measures of college environment obtained from use of the AI and the CCI.

To state the relationships found will require some explanation of the terms and methodology of George Stern's work with the AI and CCI. The terms come in two sets:

1. Environments (as measured by the CCI) emphasizing

    (a) Personal Growth, in that institutional processes contribute to the personal growth or self-actualization of participants;

---

[9] The work reported here was done by G. Stern.

      (b) Organizational Stability, in that processes are stressed which are important to the perpetuation of the institution itself; and

      (c) Impulse Control, in that there is a high level of constraint of students, with a high degree of administrative control.

2. Campus Cultures (as measured by both the AI and CCI) treated as falling on two axes:

    (a) An Intellectual–Vocational Axis

    (b) A Protective–Collegiate/Expressive Axis.

These five "cultures" can be described briefly as follows:

Collegiate. This culture emphasizes play, close policing of behavior (low dignity accorded students), and a low press for academic achievement. It stresses social form somewhat less than play and custodial care and shows a low degree of academic organization. Students in this culture show friendliness and self-assertion. Highest scorers on this culture have been large universities.

Vocational. This culture has a strong vocational press, consisting of practicality, puritanism, deference, orderliness, and adaptiveness, suggesting a high degree of conventionality and authoritarian structure. Egoism and self-assertion characterize the students (who characteristically show narcissism, fantasied achievement, and projectivity, and who score high on exhibitionistic and manipulative items). Applied studies predominate in the vocational cultures.

Protective. This culture is high in supervisory closeness. The environment scores high on group life, social form, academic organization, and self-expression; students score high on closeness, submissiveness, timidity, orderliness, and sensuousness and score low on self-assertion. Most protective cultures identified have been denominational colleges, chiefly but not exclusively women's colleges, characterized by a highly organized, supportive environment and a relatively dependent and submissive student body.

Intellectual. This culture has students with high intellectual interests and motivation and an environment of high aspiration level, intellectual press, and academic climate, with significant further characteristics favoring self-expression, vocational climate, and academic achievement. Colleges high on this culture are primarily elite liberal arts colleges but have included state universities, an engineering college, and a small Catholic women's college. Colleges low on this culture tend to be those with technical programs in business administration, engineering, and teacher training.

Expressive. This culture is low on vocational climate—a non-work-oriented, nonconforming climate, peopled by students with nonapplied interests and disinclined toward orderliness. There are scores on expressiveness, sensuousness, and friendliness. The culture is esthetic, gregarious, and nonpractical in its preoccupations, with decidedly feminist overtones. The tone suggests a community of self-actualizing, but not necessarily creative, people. Colleges scoring high on this culture are primarily elite women's colleges but include some outstanding coeducational liberal arts colleges, some large university-affiliated programs, and some Catholic women's colleges. Low scoring colleges have included a Catholic women's college and several other denominational colleges.[10]

The credence to be given these terms should rest upon an understanding of the method of analyzing student responses to the AI and CCI. The responses are subjected to factor analysis to discover (as explained on page 55 with reference to the PIQ) the smallest number of groupings of responses to account for the greatest proportion of responses. Once these groupings are found in this inductive way, the researcher studies the makeup and weighting of the items in each group for hints as to what characterizes the grouping. The name he attaches to each such grouping is a hypothesis or speculation about its characteristics.

According to Exhibit 12 there is a significant negative relationship between male college environments conducive to personal growth and the reporting of problems with faculty or students as resources. Men at the most selective liberal arts colleges, in other words, reported fewer problems with the kinds of students and staff to be found there than did men in other types of colleges. Male colleges characterized by high impulse control, however, reported problems with financial and physical resources significantly more frequently than did others. In these colleges (with high impulse control) male students reported more than at most colleges problems with the quality of faculty and fellow students

---

[10] These descriptions of cultures are paraphrased from Stern, 81.

Exhibit 12

Relations Between Problems Reported by Male Students and Characteristics of the College Environment and Culture (Pre-Interview Questionnaire, 1967)

(N = 17 Programs)

	I	II	I. Institutional resources			II. Interpersonal processes		
			1—Physical and financial resources	6—Faculty and students as resources	3—Social, esthetic and intellectual resources	2—Decision making: social and political behavior	5—Educational milieu	4—Decision making: academic affairs
Environment (CCI)*								
I. Personal growth	—.31	—.21	—.24	.50*	—.17	—.09	—.18	—.27
II. Organizational stability	—.28	—.24	—.27	—.02	—.33	.06	—.29	—.34
III. Impulse control	.47*	—.12	.23	.58**	.47*	—.21	—.18	.11
Culture (AI X CCI)*								
I. Intellectual-vocational axis	—.16	—.08	—.19	—.32	—.01	—.10	—.02	—.13
II. Protective-collegiate/expressive axis	—.01	—.19	—.09	.11	.00	—.04	—.28	—.11

* <.05   ** <.01
*** CCI = College Characteristics Index
　　AI = Activities Index

and also recorded, more than most, problems with resources for social, esthetic, and intellectual activities.

Only one significant correlation was found among these relationships for women students (Exhibit 13). Women attending denominational colleges reported fewer problems of physical plant and financial resources than women at either selective liberal arts colleges or large, collegiate universities. (On Exhibit 15 this relationship shows as a negative correlation between "Protectiveness" and frequency of reported problems of physical and financial resources.)

Four statistically significant findings occurred between faculty responses on the Pre-Interview Questionnaire and student responses to the Activities Index and College Characteristics Index on the same campuses (Exhibit 14). High personal-growth schools (selective liberal arts) were least likely to show high frequency of faculty checking of problems in decision making in academic affairs. The faculty of colleges characterized by high organizational self-maintenance (either denominational colleges or large universities) reported fewer problems than other faculties with institutional resources. More specifically, physical and financial resources and facilities for social, esthetic and intellectual activities were least likely to be reported as problems by faculty of such schools. Finally, institutions with high impulse control had fewer faculty reports of problems on decision making on social and political behavior than did others.

Administrators at high personal-growth schools reported more than their share of concerns about social and political behavior(Exhibit 15). Those at schools with high institutional stability reported fewer such problems. These schools, in fact, were regarded generally by their administrators as having fewer problems, whether interpersonal or institutional. This less frequent checking applied both to matters of physical and financial resources and to social-esthetic-intellectual resources. At high impulse control schools the administrators reported fewer interpersonal problems and fewer problems with decisions concerning political and social behavior. Administrators also found less to report on social and political behavior in Protective (denominational) cultures, and more to report on these problems in schools with a high score on the Intellectual dimension of campus culture.

In speculating on the bearing of these relationships on governance, it is important to avoid pejorative judgments which rate the campus cultures as flatly "better" or "worse" on the basis of

Exhibit 13

Relations Between Problems Reported by Female Students and Characteristics of the College Environment and Culture (Pre-Interview Questionnaire, 1967)

(N = 18 Programs)

			I. Institutional resources			II. Interpersonal processes		
	I	II	1—Physical and financial resources	6—Faculty and students as resources	3—Social, esthetic and intellectual resources	2—Decision making: social and political behavior	5—Educational milieu	4—Decision making: academic affairs
Environment (CCI)								
I. Personal growth	−.08	−.16	−.15	−.21	.10	−.05	−.17	−.19
II. Organizational stability	−.25	−.08	−.07	−.19	−.32	.01	−.06	−.15
III. Impulse control	−.03	−.23	−.31	−.09	.23	−.18	−.25	−.17
Culture (AI X CCI)								
I. Intellectual-vocational axis	.00	−.19	−.14	−.14	.21	−.11	−.19	−.19
II. Protective-collegiate/expressive axis	−.34	−.32	−.44*	−.34	−.12	−.29	−.25	−.36

* $<.05$
** CCI = College Characteristics Index
  AI = Activities Index

Exhibit 14

Relations Between Problems Reported by Faculty and Characteristics of the College Environment and Culture (Pre-Interview Questionnaire, 1967)

(N = 19 Programs)

	I	II	I. Institutional resources			II. Interpersonal processes		
			1—Physical and financial resources	6—Faculty and students as resources	3—Social, esthetic and intellectual resources	2—Decision making: social and political behavior	5—Educational milieu	4—Decision making: academic affairs
Environment (CCI)***								
I. Personal growth	.08	—.22	.10	—.05	.21	.26	—.23	—.39*
II. Organizational stability	—.41*	—.03	—.42*	—.18	—.54***	—.32	.03	.06
III. Impulse control	—.16	—.01	—.29	—.09	.15	—.43*	.00	.21
Culture (AI X CCI)***								
I. Intellectual-vocational axis	—.16	—.19	.20	—.04	.31	.22	—.20	—.36
II. Protective-collegiate/expressive axis	—.13	.12	—.21	—.01	—.08	—.27	.16	.26

* <.05   ** <.01
*** CCI = College Characteristics Index
    AI = Activities Index

Exhibit 15

Relations Between Problems Reported by Administrators and Characteristics of the College Environment and Culture (Pre-Interview Questionnaire, 1967)

(N = 19 Programs)

	I	II	I. Institutional resources			II. Interpersonal processes		
			1—Physical and financial resources	6—Faculty and students as resources	3—Social, esthetic and intellectual resources	2—Decision making: social and political behavior	5—Educational milieu	4—Decision making: academic affairs
Environment (CCI)***								
I. Personal growth	.14	.20	.19	.03	.09	.49*	.11	—.02
II. Organizational stability	—.49*	.37*	—.44*	—.30	—.54***	—.56**	—.23	—.23
III. Impulse control	—.26	.42*	—.37	—.25	.03	—.50*	—.35	—.27
Culture (AI X CCI)***								
I. Intellectual-vocational axis	.32	.20	.33	.16	.32	.48*	.17	—.05
II. Protective-collegiate/expressive axis	—.25	—.32	—.29	—.17	—.16	—.49*	—.20	—.19

* <.05   ** <.01
*** CCI = College Characteristics Index
　　　AI = Activities Index

the labeling of their cultures. Colleges with different purposes probably require different cultures, in the sense the term is used here, if they are to do their respective tasks with the greatest effectiveness. These different cultures in turn probably function best with different leadership styles. We have already noted not only the correlations reported in Highlight 10, but also those on identification of informed and influential people in Highlight 9. While the relationships found in the campuses studied here should not be assumed to be ideal, they may begin to indicate the types of differences that are likely to be effective for the differently constituted campuses.

In responding to the Activities Index and College Characteristics Index, students indicated what they liked and were like (yielding data interpreted as defining their "need") and what their campus environments were like (yielding data on the conditions and influences of that environment, or its "press"). Student perceptions of the same campus environment differed, of course, the differences being partly in the eyes of the beholders, but not entirely. The variation of reported perceptions (variance of culture scores) *within* each school in the Campus Governance Program was significantly smaller than the variation *between* schools. This finding held among private independent colleges, denominational liberal arts colleges, university-affiliated liberal arts colleges, and business, engineering, and teacher-training colleges. On the other hand, the variation among need scores of students within a given campus was nearly twice as large as that of their scores for the press of the same campus. For example, students expressing various degrees of need for intellectual stimulation found the perceived levels of stimulation less varied than their needs. What should the relationship between the two (need and press) be in an ideal learning environment? An answer raises controversial assumptions, but a plausible view would be that on such a need as intellectual stimulation the press should equal or exceed the expressed need and should not be so severe as to incapacitate the student. This hypothesis would suggest a range of presses as most suitable for a college with a wide range of student needs. The Campus Governance Program data included data on two campuses which had used the AI and CCI almost a decade earlier. In each the need scores had changed significantly, but the press scores had not. If it becomes possible, by these or other means, to assess the suitability of a campus environment for facilitating the learning of its students, the task of managing and governing to keep this relationship a highly effective one will become increasingly subtle and difficult.

The Campus Governance Program data on the AI and CCI were also analyzed by academic areas of the students' majors. The majors of 419 upper division men and 385 upper division women were classified in six categories: administrative and legal sciences, applied and technical studies (e.g., engineering), education, humanities, natural sciences, and social sciences. The differences in "culture scores" (as defined above, pages 91-92) between areas were significant for both sexes. In general, administrative and legal science majors were typified by Collegiate culture; the applied and technical studies (engineering) by Vocational; humanities and social sciences by Expressive; education by a mix of Collegiate, Vocational, and Protective; and natural science by scores close to the center on all of the axes, and undifferentiable. (Our limited sample blurs the significance of this finding; there was no distinctly Protective culture within the group, and only one clearly Expressive culture.) This information bears upon the speculation about the meaning of the frequency of problems identified, as reported in the earlier highlights.

When the Campus Governance data on the AI and CCI were grouped by public and private control, campus culture differences again emerged. The public institutions reflected much more Collegiate emphasis than did the private ones. The women's private college sample appeared more Expressive than the men's, as in an earlier larger sample studied by Stern. In these findings the differences between campuses were less a matter of differences of student need than differences of institutional inputs. Particularly for the women in public institutions, the environments were reported as clearly Collegiate, whereas the students reflected an averaging of the various types of need. The young women, in other words, were a more diversified group of personalities than were their schools as environments: the colleges in the public sample have become specialized for reasons other than a matching of their incumbent students' needs.

Finally, Stern investigated the degree and sources of dispersion of scores on the environmental characteristics studied. The degree of dispersion around the means may be viewed as a measure of cultural heterogeneity of an institution. Suppose, for example, that it were hypothesized that a highly productive learning environment would have congenial subcultures for students with different needs, but that, for best learning, these subcultures would have to interact actively with others. The campuses studied showed relatively little heterogeneity in this sense. To achieve such heterogeneity and still be productive of learning could be expected to produce great conflict and controversy. The constituencies would have different needs and priorities, different styles of living, different ways of expressing themselves and pursuing their intellectual goals.

Putting together all of the types of data reported in this chapter suggests that colleges may face an inescapable dilemma: Conflict and controversy, including the competing of diverse interests whose fulfillments are mutually interfering, may be essential to optimal learning conditions. Though such conflict need not break into violence or disruption, unskillful management or unfortunate intrusion of external forces may precipitate a destructive turn of events. A key part of the task of leadership thus becomes that of understanding these internal and external forces well enough to anticipate and prevent such a turn of events.

To those who would govern, each campus presents a unique environment with distinctive constituents. Their perceptions of problems converge in some matters, diverge in others. Their objectives and needs differ, both within a campus and between campuses. Although some helpful generalizations emerge from the study of the problems and environments of different campuses, the particular environment, constituents, objectives, and perceptions of a campus must be understood if its governance is to be what it should be. This is not to say, however, that no widely applicable guidelines for the improvement of governance can be found. The search for such guidelines is undertaken in Chapter 3.

Consent, Accountability, and Leadership

3

THE RECOMMENDATION WAS MADE IN CHAPTER 1 that institutions of higher education in America enfranchise their major constituencies more effectively. What these constituents see and say should be more fully known and heeded. But to achieve this result means difficult refinements in the ways of achieving consent, accountability, and leadership on campus.

Robert Dahl has pointed out that political influence is distributed unevenly among adult members of any political system. If the individuals with greatest political influence are called the political leaders, then every political system has them. Leaders, Dahl says, try to ensure that whenever they deal with conflict, the decisions reached are widely accepted, not solely from a fear of violence, punishment, or coercion, but also from a belief that it is morally right and proper to accept them. Widespread belief in, and commitment to, the rightness of the governing structure, processes, policies, and personnel, and acceptance of them because of this belief, give them "legitimacy." Legitimated influence is highly efficient and effective. It is more reliable and durable than influence dependent upon coercion, and it requires a minimum of political resources to be effective. In a complex and changing institution such as a college or university, in which the tasks

101

change rapidly and require a diversity of high competencies, legitimated influence is essential to institutional efficiency and effectiveness.[1]

If the importance of working agreement is granted, how can it be achieved in the substantially different settings and internal circumstances of today's campuses? How, for example, is this cardinal political principle to be applied in a complex university with over 30,000 students? in a community college in which over 80 percent of the students commute? in a small campus of 2,000 which serves subgroups of students who differ sharply in cultural background, post-college plans, philosophical orientation? in a medium-sized university with geographically scattered branches serving different age groups and vocational interests? Again and again the Campus Governance Program interviewers and questionnaires recorded complaints about delays in decision making or, conversely, actions taken without the desired consultation. The conviction grew among members of the staff that, while some campuses lack sufficient representation in councils and committees to achieve the needed consent of constituencies, further elaboration and formalization of committees, councils, and rules or procedure are likely to become increasingly cumbersome and self-defeating. On large campuses, in particular, this dilemma is acute: In the absence of increasingly formal representation there is likely to be more frequent occasion for charges of government without representation. With the proliferation of such representation and a growing problem of representatives' sustaining their constituents' adherence and confidence, there are likely to be increasing charges of co-optation and betrayal or increasing delays in action at a time when change is essential to effectiveness. What policies and practices, then, offer some promise of enabling campuses to achieve or to sustain the legitimation which effectiveness requires that they maintain?

CONSENT OF CAMPUS CONSTITUENCIES

Six observations about the meaning of consent and its achievement on campus have emerged from our reflections. They deal with consensus, unanimity, and working agreement; the when and where of consent (decentralization); consent for predictable

---

[1] Robert A. Dahl. *Modern Political Analysis.* Englewood Cliffs, N.J.: 1963. pp. 10, 16-17.

and flexible program; relationships between consent, competence, and stake; consent in feeling and idea; and the possibilities for mutually productive collaboration among those who disagree on some crucial concerns. A campus' decisions on the application of these six sets of observations to its own practices can form a program for change toward a more effective enfranchisement of its diverse constituencies.

Consensus, Unanimity, and Working Agreement

American campuses have probably never had unanimity of prime objectives among administrators, trustees, faculty, and students. Doubtless, some colleges with sectarian unity, charismatic leadership, or a special sense of educational mission were able for periods of years to sustain a good working collaboration. Autocratic leadership seems to have been easier to impose a century or more ago than now. But we cannot assert that the achievement of consensus was common or easy even then. We should best speak, perhaps, not of lost consensus, but of a present lack of adequate consensus on a growing number of campuses.

Not only should consensus not be confused with unanimity, but it should also not be equated with particular ways of determining the presence of working agreement. Quaker colleges, for instance, typically practice a rule of consensus in certain of their governing bodies because of their commitment to the "sense of the meeting" in matters of business. As practiced in an institution such as Earlham College, consensus is utterly different from unanimity. A faculty member does not make an "issue of conscience" out of every dissent he feels, and the clerk (chairman) learns to incorporate elements of minority concern into the majority resolutions in order to accord respect and influence to every possible contender.

Not only is unanimity unnecessary or unattainable in many cases, but also neither the mechanism nor the particular meaning given to consensus in such a college as Earlham is essential to the working consent which is crucial in campus governance. Some campuses which seek this working consent permit their boards and councils a routine formal vote on every major issue; others vote whenever the chairman senses that action is essential, unanimity is too cumbersome to insist upon, and the minority is ready to cooperate but not to record assent. This last pattern may be preferable to formal consensus in a community without experience in formal consensus, or without developed skill in knowing when individual concern should yield to majority judgment, or simply not schooled to a tradition of votes that mean agreement to cooperate rather than enthusiasm about the content of the minute. Thus in selecting a new president, the College of St. Thomas recently achieved the effect of consensus while preserving the form of election by the board of trustees. The archbishop, who was chairman of the board, accomplished this result by consulting the faculty and others with a quality of listening no different from that of the best Quaker clerks.

Even campuses like Earlham, however, had at the time of our observations (with Earlham this occurred in 1967 [2]) not yet extended to students the franchise on the most fundamental campus policies. None of the campuses studied had enfranchised nonfaculty staff even on the matters of most direct concern to them, except through the mechanism of unionization on some of the larger campuses. While formal enfranchisement is no more necessary to the achievement of a workable form of consent than is formal consensus, its absence is generally a signal that the unenfranchised group is not recognized as a constituency as here recommended.

Working agreement can be facilitated by attention to the timing of decision processes, their content, the different contributions possible for different constituents, the role of feeling and idea in agreement, and the division of labor and approach to authority sharing among constituencies.

Consent at Different Times and Places (Decentralization)

In order for campus administrators to combine prompt, efficient action with adequate concern for consent of campus constituencies revision of prevailing ideas about "consent of the governed" is necessary. The first needed revision in thinking about consent of the governed is to add a specification as to the time to obtain consent. On some matters, consent should be obtained in advance of action; on others, afterward will suffice; and on still others, consent should be checked out both before, during, and after action. In the choice of president a number of campuses visited had increased, within the past decade, the role of faculty, students, or other constituents in the processes of nomination, screening, and recommendation for appointment. These are ways

---

[2] Keeton, 62.

of eliciting consent in advance of commitment. A study of presidential selection procedures cites such developments with approval and further recommends that some form of periodic review of the president's performance be used.[3]

Changes are also under way in the making of budgets. As budgets have grown larger and more complex and as the contingencies, errors of estimate, and needs to institute changes of program between biennial or annual budget adoption dates have increased, the need for more continuous review and revision of budgets has grown. This need, in turn, creates difficulties in securing and sustaining constituents' understanding and consent. To master the detail and to debate the many significant issues involved in a line-by-line budget of even a moderately complex campus can overload faculty or student representatives as well as state legislators. If, on the other hand, they participate in making the budget without thorough understanding, the quality of decisions suffers. Besides, detailed and unalterable fixing of the budget hampers later problem solving. However, to permit administrators the discretion to change budgets later without limiting that authority or subjecting it to periodic review is to risk the disadvantages of autocratic management and lost consensus. For these reasons more and more campuses are trying to find ways of accommodating the requirements of good problem solving to the demands of political legitimacy in budget tending and vice versa. A key tactic in achieving the accommodation is the division of labor in consent-sustaining activities between tasks best done in advance of appropriation and those best done after the operating year is under way.

The sophistication thus achieved in making and revising budgets and in selecting and retaining presidents has generally not been applied to the conduct of curricular affairs and other aspects of campus governance and management. Once it is granted that consent is best obtained at different times on different issues, we must ask: How can the interplay of consent maintenance and effective management be improved through a division of effort among "pre-audits" (advance consent), "continuous audits" (periodic review during operation), and "post-audits" (appraisal after action as a guide to future decisions)?

---

[3] Frederick deW. Bolman. "How Will You Find a College President?" *Journal of Higher Education* 36: 200-08; April 1965.

In the complex organizations that more and more campuses are becoming, a pre-audit of every important program, policy, and personnel decision becomes extremely expensive, cumbersome, and frustrating to both managers and constituents. On some of the campuses visited the detailed requirement of pre-audit of curricular decisions (e.g., required plenary faculty, senate, or committee approval of every major course change, or committee approval of each student's degree program) was regarded by student and faculty critics as a way in which entrenched faculty or administrator groups frustrated a majority sentiment for change. Whatever the merits of the charge, the governance process forced an erosion of working agreement. To avoid such frustrations, some campuses had allowed ways to develop for evading the clogged channels for approval; for example, overlapping jurisdictions between different committees made it possible for a group to choose the channel most likely to act promptly and favorably. But these arrangements also contribute to a sense of lost legitimacy and weakened consensus. Timing of decision and allocation of different types of decision to different stages of effort are by no means a complete answer to these difficulties. Some of the difficulties are traceable to inadequate recognition of the rights and competencies of some of the constituencies in deciding the types of issues in question. (This type of problem is discussed in the section Consent and Competence To Govern, below.)

Some campuses have eased the frustrations of advance consent by adopting efficiencies in decision making. For example, on some campuses hearings before legislative action permitted wider participation in debate without causing the formal legislative meetings to become ensnarled in interminable and unorganized discussion or in endless parliamentary maneuvering. The usefulness of this strategy for expediting decisions, however, is probably greater in improving the atmosphere of consent and the quality of decisions than in reducing the load of decision making.

Some campus administrators and constituency leaders have sought to anticipate the interests of their constituents and to fulfill those interests without involving the constituents directly in debate and decision making. This is a key to the effectiveness of the benevolent autocrat in administration, who was found on more than one campus, and of some of the entrenched student or faculty leaders identified by respondents to our Pre-Interview

Questionnaire. This type of sensitivity, if not turned into a habit of bending to any breeze, is an important qualification for leadership as defined by Dahl. However, as one interviewer commented, it can become a "sophisticated guessing game which gives administrators (or other leaders) all sorts of room for doing what *they* want with the defense that they *tried* to anticipate others' needs." It is, then, an element of good governance that continues to have a good effect only if checked by adequate processes of audit by the constituents.

A further device for reconciling the requirements of working agreement with those of practicality is reflected in the budget-managing processes already mentioned. This is a form of decentralization, in which decisions of different types and scopes are made by different units of management or policy making; this decentralization of effort then permits those most concerned with detail to have the full authority to decide upon the detail within the broad limits set by those who represent broader institutional interests. The division of labor between those who set broad policy and those who control smaller programs or units of the campus is set in advance by those with broad jurisdictions. Those who are thus accorded control of component programs or units may, in turn, decide what matters within their endeavor should be handled by pre-audit, continuous audit, or post-audit. Sometimes this type of decentralization is accompanied by provision for the broad policy makers to conduct a post-audit of the performance of those to whom authority and jurisdiction were delegated. The post-audit may also be done by sampling or selective probes rather than by a comprehensive study if a reliable and valid way of selective probing can be devised.

Universities have long experience with some types of decentralization. Colleges and institutes are common units to which jurisdiction is granted, and within them departments or divisions often achieve substantial degrees of autonomy. These arrangements permit those most committed to the college, institute, department, or division to put more time into the work with which they are most concerned than if all policies and programs had to be cleared with higher authorities. The leaders of the smaller units thus have greater freedom to do their work in the ways they judge best than if their plans had to be approved by further councils or administrators. This decentralization, however, entails a risk for others. If the campus is to be more than an aggregate of quite separate organizations which are only nominally one institution, then the problem of maintaining working agreement, mutual commitment, and mutual trust and respect exists here as well as in more centralized institutions.

Decentralization introduces not only a division of labor on a time scale, but also a division of labor as to the locus of deciding. This, in turn, affects the options as to who may take part in what decisions. (This question will be treated further in the section Consent and Competence To Govern, below.) The assignment of different decisions to different times and loci, however, calls for recognition of a further complication in the meaning of consent of the governed and sharing of authority. In some matters the sharing takes the form of joint participation in deciding. In others it takes the form of agreeing that different parties will within defined limits make the decisions alone. Both types of sharing were employed in what seemed to interviewers the most effective practices of the campuses studied.

There seems to be a greater openness on many campuses today than a decade ago toward the use of decentralization and differently timed procedures of audit and consent. This openness arises in part out of a desire to have smaller subcommunities or "consent groups" so less time goes into councils and committees ("into machinery," in one phrasing) and more into teaching or research and service, and individualized programs are possible without spending inordinate effort in getting advance approval. This sentiment thus fits the concern for individualization of program, for community, and for subordinating bureaucratic activities to program activities.

There are, however, enormous difficulties in diversifying the patterns of timing in seeking constituents' consent. Most people prefer or demand to be "asked in advance" about matters which they construe as vital. Our traditions are generally against "asking after things are under way." In state-controlled systems of higher education it is not within the control of the residents of a campus to shift many of the presently pre-audited types of decisions to a different timing. When the shift has been made and freedom has been given to innovate and individualize, some who obtained the discretionary authority have overspent their authorizations, some have failed to generate the needed resources for their own tasks, and some have been perceived as fostering ventures that undermined standards or subverted the purposes which the institution professed. In other words, the problems generated by introducing variety into the timing and locus of decision making may present a new order of magnitude of difficulty, even greater than that of presently prevailing practices. Who shall do the post-audits? How can competence to do continuous or delayed appraisals be combined with credibility of the monitors in the eyes of the consenting constituents? Will there be constant added controversy about the proper time and place for the many different types of decision? Such question will complicate new patterns of decision making.

There is, on the other hand, hardly a choice as to whether to explore these more complex arrangements for sustaining consent and legitimation for the purposes, programs, and policies of the campuses. In a recent report, for example, the president of Harvard University attributed much of the strength of the institution to its policy that "each tub must stand upon its own bottom"—a policy of decentralizing fiscal responsibility to colleges and institutes within overall university guidelines. A contrasting pattern of "collegiality" in decision making on curricular change has been blamed by Dwight R. Ladd for the sluggish and disappointing achievement of the most reputable innovating institutions examined in his study *Change in Educational Policy*. For proper consideration of even the basic goals and objectives, he says,

> it was simply not possible . . . to take the amount of time the task required. Beyond these matters is the question of whether or not such large numbers of people—each with an equal voice—could be brought to face such fundamental issues in a productive way, even if structure and time were provided. Given the extreme diversity of interests and activity of these faculty members and their varying degrees of attachment to their particular institutions, it is not surprising that the collegial system has not, in these cases, worked very well.

He proposes alternative approaches to solving the problems of policy making thus posed. One is to subdivide or otherwise create "institutions which are neither too large nor too diverse and where the character and objectives . . . are relatively well understood and accepted by its members." The other is "the development of a system akin to the responsible government of the parliamentary democracies" where power to decide is given to leaders who must consult effectively or lose their mandate.[4]

---

[4] Dwight R. Ladd. *Change in Educational Policy*. New York: McGraw-Hill Book Co., 1970. pp. 214ff.

The problems of these new efforts to restore the sense of legitimation on campuses will surely not be less complex than those of the past, but they should be the problems inherent in doing better the things which the campus constituencies aspire to have done. There seems to be no reasonable alternative to tackling these problems.

Consent to Predictable but Flexible Program

A further needed revision in the concept of consent of the governed on campus has to do with the ways in which agreement about goals, programs, and policies is reached and recognized. The same interviewees on campus after campus wanted, on one issue, to get a firm agreement in writing out of the authorities and, on another issue, to be free of the prevailing bureaucratic insistence upon the letter of the policy. There is no necessary inconsistency in this juxtaposition of concerns on different issues. The example points, however, to an additional source of tension in governance for which improved practices are needed. There is, on the one hand, the need for clarity, definiteness, and predictability in policy and practice. There is, on the other hand, the need for flexibility and capability of prompt and adaptive change when circumstances or purposes change. It is difficult enough to find an effective accommodation of these needs in the eyes of a single constituency, such as the faculty. The difficulty is compounded when the perceptions of trustees, legislators, alumni, students, parents, and staff must also be reconciled.

Most campuses probably err by coupling in their rhetoric an excessive deference for written agreements with inattentiveness in their day-to-day operations to the compliance of action with written resolution. The campuses studied supplied a wealth of documents on purposes, policies, and manuals of procedures. In councils and committees these were often cited and had to be amended before change could be sanctioned. The practices under way at the same time often differed substantially from what was written in the documents. This disparity between profession and practice is nothing new, of course; nor is it altogether avoidable. But it infuriates those who see it as obstructing needed change. The point of again focusing upon it is to ask why it persists and what better can be done.

A major source of tension between settled policy (often represented in documents) and day-to-day practice is the heavy pressure of our times toward enlargement and diversification of the purposes of a campus. In any given year a great many colleges experience significant dissatisfaction with their current articulation of mission. The response of campuses visited to the recent interest in "black studies" is a case in point. The demands often were athwart established policies on admission standards and procedures, curricular policies and approval processes, and even policies on civil rights and integration. To sort out, with reasonable approximation to working agreement among constituents, the merits of these many demands and to do so with sufficient speed to be responsive to the depth and importance of the concerns was an agonizing experience for at least two of the campuses studied.

Agreements on goals, programs, and policies are elements of self-definition. Self-definition is fundamentally not a matter of written expressions, but of commitments of work and life. Written expressions can facilitate the achievement of clarity, congruity, and wisdom in the choice of these commitments. Often, however, the changes just cited are not matched by updating of the written and unwritten understandings of the campus. Different leaders may recognize this lag and have their own perceptions of the appropriate adjustments in understanding, but there is no assurance that they agree among themselves in these perceptions, that their constituencies would sanction these interpretations and adjustments if asked, or that closer study would sustain their judgment of how to adapt earlier purpose to present conditions. Reference was made in Chapter 2 to George Stern's comparison of the culture of 1967 with that of 1959 on two campuses. On each of them the student need reflected in questionnaire responses had changed more markedly than the campus environment. The role of "preserving and enhancing the intellectual functions in the culture" persists as a key element of purpose on each campus, but the styles and modes of intellectuality among students have shifted so that the specific meaning of this purpose for teaching, learning, and public service should also be reconsidered if the college is to succeed in its intent.

How can a campus give less homage to earlier formulations of purpose, program, and policy and at the same time pay more attention to keeping them revised? How can respect for institutional heritage, with the strength and focusing of effort that result, be combined with openness to the doubting and reshaping of that heritage? Listening to and observing diverse campuses caught in this tension, we could see that commitments of program and purpose are never complete in specificity, especially if they affect many people over much time and are carried out with great effectiveness.

Within their intellectual role in human culture, campus purposes can best be thought of as a cluster of functions, some having to do with the development of students, some with the generation of knowledge, some with service to a further constituency, and some with the pursuit of certain further intellectual, religious, or social convictions. While some of a campus' functions can and should be deliberately chosen, others may remain latent, fulfilled more or less inadvertently. Not many faculty prize their colleges because of their usefulness in delaying marriage and in effective matchmaking, or because of their part in getting individuals of different and potentially hostile subcultures to appreciate each other and to work together. Yet these unadvertised functions should be more explicitly accepted and stated. They may be among the major contributions of higher education to the strength and productivity of our society, and they may have intellectual import beyond that of some of the more honored collegiate tasks.

Consent in self-definition is further complicated by the fact that some elements in a college's purpose appear to be, and may be, at odds with others—vocational preparation with liberal education in a college for women, pastoral theology with theological debate in a Catholic men's college, research in controversial territories with the protection of academic freedom, etc. These cross-purposes may stimulate a college and reinforce each other if properly managed and pursued in a context of consensus on broadly shared aims and attitudes. But they do not make for clear and unambiguous prose in the grasp and statement of mission. The focus on verbal formulations of purpose and program can end in agreement about words among people who differ in intent or in disagreement about words among people who seek fundamentally congruent ends. More fruitful as a means of continuing self-definition of a campus by its constituencies may be a combination of efforts to record agreements of this kind with other efforts at assessing the outlays of both energy and money in various tasks. In the section Accounting to the Consenters, below, we will discuss some of the ways that this ongoing consideration and review can occur.

Even with the best of aids, however, self-definition of a campus with general consent is likely to become increasingly difficult.

Disagreements are likely to become more numerous and significant. Often agreement will be possible only with essential change.
We are adept at relabeling and repackaging the same old cereal.
We are as resistant as the next people to changing a basic recipe—
all honestly and with good reasons. "We tried that ten years
ago." "The wrong change is proposed." "The idea is good, but
it won't work as expected." "The idea is good, but you can't do
it without destroying the quality of what we are already doing."
"There is not enough time to get ready." "There are problems in
it that we do not know how to resolve." The critics are often right.
To get the information needed and yet to get on with the choices,
a campus must develop faculty, student, and administrative leaders who can deal with emerging facts and forces, not by strong-
arm tactics, but by listening, questioning, considering and recon-
sidering, and finally deciding and acting. Such leaders run the
risk of being repudiated later, for the constituencies may consent
to such leadership only if they can change it when their intent
has been misread.

Consent and Competence To Govern

Chapter 1 indicated a number of contributions to a campus' governance which different constituencies can make. To obtain these
various contributions in an optimum combination, however, is
not easy. There are costs and hazards in trying. The potential of
a campus using its faculty, staff, student, and administrator competences in governing may be far greater than that of a less
democratically conducted campus; but to govern in this way is
clearly more complex and difficult in the short run than the usual
ways. Only campuses that invest substantially in this more complex effort can realize that potential.

The unwillingness of those in power to share authority was a
key difficulty on many campuses in the effort to broaden the
input to decision making. The 1966-67 Task Force on Faculty
Representation reported cases in which forms of participation
were used, but the president was unwilling to permit a senate
or council to be made up or to function in ways that might produce decisions different from those he would otherwise have
made. On other campuses faculty took a similar attitude toward
student voice in curricular or faculty personnel matters.

The unwillingness of constituents to trust their peers as
representatives or leaders was another obstacle to effectively
shared authority. Many causes can aggravate this problem: the

belief that administrators are outwitting or using the nonadmin-
istrative representatives; the use of appointed representatives
rather than elected ones; the tendency for representatives to become more knowledgeable than their constituents, to fail to keep
the constituents informed, and thus to lose touch; failure of
representatives to express the diversity of views and concerns
among their peers; belief that the faculty or student representatives are more interested in personal advancement than in the
causes and concerns of their constituents; a piling of up unresolved issues; etc. Many of the "reforms" of the 1960's placed
small minorities of students on what were formerly faculty committees with the intent of giving students a voice but preserving
faculty control. Though effective in maintaining faculty control,
these moves often convinced many students that the majority of
faculty had no intention of sharing authority and that students
who accepted the committee roles were suspect. This charge of
"tokenism" often worked against the effectiveness of these committees. Sometimes the critique shifted from the representatives
to the very concept of representation.

A third source of difficulty with enlarged participation in
governance is that it was sometimes sought and granted for
wrong reasons, with the result that the expectations embedded
in these wrong reasons were thereby confirmed, while the more
productive bases for shared authority were prevented from working. For example, the opportunity to influence decision and action
was often granted because of awareness that the dissenters or
petitioners could interfere or do damage unless given a say. This
danger is real, of course; and at times there is no better alternative than to accede to it. If, however, a campus takes on the
climate that the ability to threaten harm is the most effective
way to achieve influence, the chances are reduced for decision
making that is informed by the thoughtful weighing of different
and sometimes conflicting constituents' perspectives.

A fourth difficulty with sharing authority with diverse constituencies lies in the problems of providing time and resources
for senates, council, and committees to do their work well. On
some campuses a newly instituted council was immediately con-
fronted with an unmanageably long or detailed agenda, and this
type of overload was not uncommon for long-established councils
on campuses that had grown larger and more complex during the
past decade. The move toward representative councils can fall
into excessive reliance upon councils, voting, and representatives

in the communication and effectuation of constituents' concerns. Some campuses try to meet the demands for time of representatives by limiting the committee obligations of faculty, reducing other duties for faculty representatives, and putting administrative staff time and office services at the disposal of the representatives. Some campuses make heavy use of ad hoc committees or task groups to reduce the load on key bodies in their governing structures.

A fifth source of concern about governing groups of mixed constituencies was how to persuade to serve and to get elected those persons best qualified. This concern is complicated by the fact that the different types of qualification rarely come in ideal combination. For example, the student with greatest charisma in cementing student commitment to council decisions may be relatively ineffective in winning faculty and administrative support for his valid concerns.

A further example of the complexities of trying to get the best effect of the interplay of many competences in a campus governing body is that of an inherent tension in the representation of competing interests. Some of these competing interests are built into the university's own purposes. A faculty representative is at one time a teacher, a researcher, and possibly a specialist in some form of intellectually based public service. He is further specialized as to task and discipline. The priorities of these various interests compete with one another and with his task as representative to see to the general well-being of his institution. Professors and students are no more immune to conflicts of interest and parochialism of perspective than other human beings. In making salary budgets, faculty members are parties at interest; in holding down tuitions, students are parties at interest. The parochialism of the faculty is in part that of the expert, who often overestimates the importance of that aspect of a choice to which his expertise is most pertinent. The parochial interest of the expert may appear in subtle forms, such as the effect of a change in degree requirements upon the enrollments in introductory courses, which eventually affect the number of majors in a department and its appropriations for facilities, equipment, and faculty. A major reason for shared authority arrangements is, of course, to counterbalance the biases of governance in which only one or some of the interests and perspectives that should apply are represented. Putting one bias against another, however, is of limited use unless the encounter can stimulate an examination of reasons for the opposing views and of alternatives to their recommendations.

The data of our Nineteen Campus Study show that the interest of students in a voice in governance varies more widely from campus to campus than does that of faculty. There was also much less agreement across the country as to the legitimate roles or voice of students in governance than for faculty. Major discrepancies in expectations on these points on the same campus can signal trouble for plans to share authority. For example, the great majority of students on one campus expected to be able to contribute creative new ideas about course offerings and to have many of them adopted, whereas faculty leaders there were equally unanimous in expecting to persuade students on councils that their ideas were premature or unfeasible. This campus might better organize separate student and faculty curriculum committees, with the latter in explicit control, rather than a joint student–faculty committee making a pretense of seeking consensus. Four questions are involved here in the choice of ways to accommodate the different student, faculty, and administrator concerns in authority sharing:

1. On what matters does each constituency (students, faculty, administrators, trustees, or other combinations of those who seek influence) want a voice, and what voice does it want on each matter?

2. On what matters do others of the campus community urge that the desired sharing of authority take place, and in what form?

Since complete congruity among the answers to these two questions will be rare, provision has to be made for contested or negotiated allocations of responsibility. The manner of contesting these matters should not destroy the climate of cooperation on other matters. Also, the choice as to how these responsibilities will be exercised calls attention to two further questions:

3. What expectations and perceptions do campus groups have as to how they will function in their governance roles?

4. What time and other resources will the individuals and the institution put into preparation for, and exercise of, the responsibilities?

This last question points to a final difficulty that emerges from the recognition of the imperfect starting qualifications of representatives in governing bodies. This problem of imperfectly qualified representatives is aggravated by the constant turnover of membership inherent in faculty, student, and other staff representation. Those who were inexperienced before they served on councils and committees typically report that they learned much during their service, and others confirm this. In fact, this byproduct of a better informed and sophisticated campus membership is one of the reasons for increasing participation in governing bodies. This very fact, however, implies that the representatives were less than ideally qualified when they began; and a process which replaces experienced spokesmen in order to renew constituency commitment and reflect new alignments of concern must continue to accentuate this difficulty.

What can be done about these costs and difficulties with the enlistment of diverse voices in campus councils? Three effective strategies were observed in use by campuses: (a) focusing efforts upon the problems of sharing authority rather than prolonging ideological debate as to whether to share; (b) making a substantial investment of time and other resources in overcoming the types of problems identified above; and (c) supplementing the use of representative committees and councils with other means of sharing influence and power.

Disagreement about the sharing of authority is rarely a matter of unconditional opposition to any and all influence or power for the disfranchised. Almost always the issue is more specific: it may be one of protecting the administration's ability to see to fiscal solvency, or one of protecting a faculty veto in matters of curriculum. Everyone will acknowledge that students do influence and should influence the makeup of curriculum by their choice of majors, electives, instructors, etc. Disagreement about changing the present opportunities, when analyzed closely, is more fruitfully tackled by the invention of alternative ways to meet the conflicting concerns than by a debate in which one or the other party defines the concerns as irreconcilable.

Similarly, we visited campuses where faculty were seeking greater authority or different ways of exercising the authority which was accepted as appropriately theirs. The best outcome of these pressures occurred where it was acknowledged that a campus simply could not function well if faculty withheld their cooperation or became demoralized by the sense that their rights and competences were not respected.

It has often been difficult, however, to get behind the controversy on a campus to the genuine fears and concerns which underlie the antagonists' arguments. Not everyone by any means will welcome an effort to transmute an ideological stalemate into a resolvable process of need definition and problem solving; but the earlier this can be done in a dispute's evolution toward confrontation, the more readily the energies of conflict can be turned to a fruitful outcome.

Once the complexity of competing concerns in sharing authority is recognized and the resolution to work with them is developing, it becomes clear that sharing authority is a time-consuming, expensive way to function. This very fact can be used as a further argument in the ideological battle and may stall action until the greater costs of not sharing loom clear. A number of campuses have suspended classes and other operations for days or set up term-long processes of increased meetings and staff-and-volunteer work to thrash out new patterns of decision making. These in turn normally call for greater time spent in deliberations of governing and greater costs in staff work, communications, and evaluation of effort. The preceding analysis of difficulties in sharing authority, however, suggests that these costs are not temporary or peripheral, but endemic and central to the requirements of such ways of governing. It seems probable that once more experience is gained with the potentials and the problems of sharing authority, the needed investment in mining those potentials will be seen to be vastly greater than even the most innovative colleges and universities have yet attempted. In fact, those who have experimented most with these devices are generally the ones for whom peculiar conditions made the venture least hazardous and least costly. The large, complex campuses working under externally imposed limitations that complicate the problems are the ones which will have the greatest need for a large investment in overcoming the problems of sharing authority.

To advocate shared authority and to warn against the limitations of representative democracy may seem paradoxical. Data about what is presently occurring, even when coupled with data on dissatisfactions and satisfactions with experiments in authority sharing, cannot tell us what to do better. A part of the meaning of the past decade's campus experiences, however, is that the conditions which make representative mechanisms effective have been exceeded on many campuses. Already reported is Ladd's recommendation that complex universities either decentralize or shift to "responsible government" patterns. These methods have the effect of making the tasks of governing manageable in size and number for the participation of the concerned and competent parties.

In addition to these two very fundamental strategies for sharing authority, there is great potential in improved use of internal research and feedback, in the use of volunteer participation in administrative and legislative tasks within the units of a decentralized system, and in informal and formal consultation in a context of responsive legislative and management operations. On a campus of 15,000 students, for example, open hearings might attract only 200 participants if held early in consideration of a potentially hot issue; and their involvement at that stage can avert an angry battle which later might attract two or three thousand with less effective input of student perspective and insight for resolution of their concerns. Or, to take another example, in the appraisal of the teaching performance of faculty members, no one in either the faculty or student body can know enough about the work of the many teachers involved in even a medium-sized campus without systematically conducted study. Only a mechanism which routinely provides this feedback, not the votes in council as such, can adequately inform the judgment of appointive authorities.

Consent in Feeling and Idea

The giving of consent is an act of both intellectual agreement and emotional commitment. Agreement on ideas does not always bring with it the force of commitment sufficient for effective action. Differences in the depth of feeling about an issue may also reflect differences in priority or disagreements about values which at the time of encounter are still unarticulated; if and when articulated, these disagreements can emerge as policy issues of a different type from those which had been under consideration before. In most organizations today, notably in colleges and universities, there is far from adequate emphasis given to the intellectual questions embedded in clashes of feeling. Similar oversight has occurred with the problems of commitment and collaboration present in verbal agreements made in the face of still unresolved reservations at the level of feeling or emotion.

An adequate policy and practice in enlisting the consent of constituents will heed at least two types of contribution implicit in
recognizing the importance of feeling in campus communications:
(a) communication of priorities and urgency of concerns; and
(b) clues to unarticulated ideas or to pre-articulate apprehension
of conceptual material. Each of these types of contribution came
to notice in the interviews and in other experiences of staff and
consultants of the Campus Governance Program.

Communication of priorities and urgency of concerns. The
priority and urgency of a concern to a significant number of constituents is highly relevant to the choice of whom to consult about
it, on what timing to develop the decision, and by what methods
of deliberation to settle the matter. Some of our interview notes
indicate that this aspect of campus communications had gone
unheard or had been rejected as not admissible for consideration.
For example, on one campus ghetto neighbors and campus activ-
ists joined in trying to get consideration of their opposition to
a projected building on adjacent community recreation land but
felt unheeded until they physically obstructed the university's
effort to build. In other cases, having to do with matters ranging
from a desired change in degree requirements to the perennial
agitation for a change in parietal rules, the student or faculty
group concerned had given up for the time being but harbored
the view that no fair process of consideration had been given
to their concern. In another case, trustees did permit an intrusion by a guerrilla theatre group with a concern about college
investment in racially discriminatory businesses. The trustees
deplored the method of expression, but responded to the importance and timeliness of the concern, and resolved the issue in a
way which, while not wholly approved by the petitioners, was
acknowledged to be responsive to their concern and fairly considered. Doubtless, it is a very small number of institutions whose
trustees could tolerate guerrilla intrusions and deal creatively
with them. There are, however, ways suited to the circumstances
and traditions of different institutions by which they can give
heed to expressions of priority and urgency of concern, even when
these expressions are relatively inarticulate. Failure to heed the
cognitive message of emotional pleas is at the base of the gulf
in some student–faculty conflicts about relevance in higher
education.

Expressions of feeling which reflect unarticulated ideas.
Even the constituents of a university are not always articulate

about some of their greatest concerns. This inarticulateness may spring from anger, frustration, or fear. Confusion of issues may cause a spokesman to put his emphasis on one point when the real concern is on another. Difficulty in articulation may arise from the different frames of reference of hearers and speakers, so that a perfectly clear message in one group's way of speaking is unintelligible to another group. The inarticulateness may be a consequence of the novelty of the insight or idea, for which no adequate vocabulary has been devised. An emotional broadside loosed at the dean's curricular policy may signal that he is viewed as too domineering; if he is, a change is in order even if his policy is sound; if he is not, some accommodation may be essential to the collaboration of an important constituency whose help is essential to the best work of the college. Our campus interviewers encountered cogent critiques from persons so frustrated by the repeated denial of their concerns that they would no longer remain courteous and apparently could no longer think of solutions acceptable to those in power. On the other hand, on at least one campus where administrators and faculty were seeking an alternative to prevalent crediting and grading systems, efforts to do away with grades and credits were at a standstill because no one could formulate convincingly an alternaitve way to define the degree. The problem may be insoluble, or it may simply be one for which those with the concern and vision are not yet able to articulate the solution.

There is a further type of circumstance in which sound criticism seems to come from the inarticulate. It is often the case that students, faculty, or outsiders with a legitimate concern do not know enough to devise a successful implementation of their own suggestion. They may simply lack access to needed information or expertise, as with faculty trying to obtain a cut in administrative costs; or they may not grasp the interplay of conflicting considerations involved in a problem, as with students attacking parietal rules but unable, when given dormitory autonomy, to provide the essential conditions for a productive and livable environment for residents. These are cases not of a defect of ability to state ideas, but of perceiving a difficulty without yet knowing a way out.

The use of emotion to override or evade adequate analysis and inquiry can, of course, damage the quality of decision making. A part of the governance problem occasioned by emotionalism in expression is the likelihood that it will meet, or even generate, unwillingness in the hearers to accept or act upon valid criticisms or proposals made in this way. For these reasons it is common in collegiate controversy to hear a critic chided for the emotional, unconstructive, and logically irrelevant character of his discourse. Critiques and proposals are also often rejected because they are not accompanied by technically adequate implementation. As a result, substantively sound criticism and suggestions are rejected because of the ground rules of unemotionalism, strict logical relevance in the terms of reference of the holders of prerogative, and the requirement that plans for implementation be supplied by the same people who advance the need for them. There are, of course, good reasons for insisting that, before adoption, the case for or against an idea meet the tests of consistency, relevance to college purpose, and practicality. It is also hardly a cure for suppressed emotions if a faculty meeting turns into a lay attempt at group therapy. Yet the idea that intellectuals are, or ought to be, less emotional than other mortals must be doubted. Some studies correlating verbal aptitude with impulsivity and unconventionality of behavior suggest that at least some highly creative groups of intellectuals have more than their share of need for impulse expression. Perhaps the ability to feel strongly about ideas is one of the virtues of the intellectual community. If this virtue could be harnessed with methods of decision making that welcome strong feeling while ensuring equally acute appraisal of the ideational content, a new potential in campus deliberations would be created.

This proposal that campus emotion be enlisted in the cause of improving governance presents peculiar difficulties for campus leaders. Some of them are often the targets of confrontation, at the focal point of polarization of feelings. At the same time others of them are normally active in creating the confrontation if it reaches the scope of campus-wide concern. For example, on one campus the insensitivity of a dean of women to student values created a confrontation in a previously unorganized student community; while on another campus student leaders deliberately agitated for a showdown with the president on a different type of issue. Someone is needed in such a situation who can translate for one constituency the relevance of criticisms and demands from another constituency's perspective. Someone is needed who can help an inarticulate concern get articulate expression, help an impractical drive take practical form, and help mutually offended factions hear and heed one another. This someone cannot always be a person in formal authority. Campus controversies often carry a heavy load of personal attack upon the campus administrators themselves. For them to apply the skills of creative conflict management under such attack is a highly demanding task.

Some of the campuses visited in 1966 and 1967 in the Campus Governance Program erupted shortly afterward in serious confrontations and disturbances; most did not. We cannot attribute the difference solely to the quality of management or leadership on the campuses that escaped disruption. In fact, few, if any, would have claimed to have an adequate conception of the criteria for creatively conducted controversy, much less to have developed the skills to implement those criteria.

Strategies of Power Sharing

That power on campus can and must be shared has been stressed already, but how can this be done with integrity for the sharers and with benefit for the campus and its society? The realities of campus and society do not permit an ideal strategy for power sharing. At the same time, these realities force a search for a strategy more creative than each group's grabbing all it can away from every other group.

In sharing a pie, if I give any to someone else, I get less as a direct result. No scheme of sharing will add to, or subtract from, the total amount of pie to be shared. Pie sharing is a *zero-sum game*. The sum of what one party loses and the others thereby gain is always zero. There are "games," ways of sharing, that work differently, activities in which one can get more by giving up some than by trying to capture everything. In business, the credit system is based upon the possibility that both lender and borrower may benefit financially by the lender's giving up certain uses of his capital and getting other benefits (interest and possibly capital gains), while the borrower is thus enabled to fund a purchase or an enterprise which, after payments to the lender, benefits him more than otherwise would have been possible. "A good reason for borrowing," as one TV ad says, "is a good reason for lending." This type of game, the *positive sum game,* is one in which each gains because he heeds the interest of the other, and together they increase the sum of benefits enjoyed by virtue of their superior understanding of mutual self-interest.

There is a third strategy of sharing power, which works more like friendship or problem solving in a common disaster. It is not a game at all in the sense of requiring each participant to play with the sole intent of maximizing his own gain. It is rather a *nongame* in which the interest of the other party becomes one of one's own interests, respect for his feelings becomes one of one's own concerns, and the conflict of ideas or exploration of options may result in the participants' altering their aims and priorities.

Only campuses that achieve in their power-sharing strategies a measure of these last two (the positive sum game and the nongame) can become outstandingly efficient and effective in the performance of their chosen functions in higher education.

The first difficulty with this finding, however, is that some campus problems seem inherently to present only zero-sum options. Take the options in making a budget when resources are stable or shrinking, as when a legislature imposes a ceiling on both appropriations and tuition charges. Such a situation tends to force the participants to vie with one another for insufficient resources. However, in most campus problems where this is so, it is because the participants choose to define the situation in this way. Consider the low-ceiling budget from a short-run and a long-run view, for example. If individuals and departments and colleges of a university are so disposed, a crisis of inadequate funds can elicit a host of ideas for sharing staff, equipment, facilities, and other resources. They can thus make short-run, if limited, progress in the objectives affected by the budget restrictions. The crisis may force a needed collaboration on campus in discovering how to achieve excellence or improvement at tolerable cost. For the longer run also, the question arises of whether the campus can achieve a positive-sum game or nongame relationship with the legislature and its other constituencies. If higher education continues to battle farmers, labor, business, etc., for the favors of the legislatures in a zero-sum strategy, the outlook for adequate resources is indeed glum. The pressure of this type of competition may have a certain grim usefulness in forcing campuses to reexamine the sources of efficiency in learning and research, but forced cuts in costs often yield counterproductive savings. Even a strategy of getting together with the other lobbies and with legislators to find ways to foster one another's interests may have limited long-run utility for higher education. The positive sum game in this context has something of the flavor of honor among thieves who, in this case, get together to fleece the taxpayer and the consumers. The sense among taxpayers and students that our society functions in this way may be at the very heart of the crisis of authority in American politics, as one of the Campus Governance Program consultants suggested. This sense of the situation may be a major focus of the tendency among students and faculty on some campuses to deny the legitimacy of the political system (i.e., to deny it their sanction and support). If so, they could hardly approve a similar strategy within the campus or between it and the rest of society.

This example of limited resources as a restraint upon the possibility of escaping zero-sum games has a further significance. The resources of our society are limited at any given time relative to the vision in our society as to the good things we could do. Wars and space flights compete with pollution control and the improvement of health. If the world succeeds in eliminating war, then education and the improvement of justice and other similar social functions will still compete with one another for inadequate resources. In the relationships of institutions of higher education to the larger society, it is increasingly likely that the magnitude of resources needed will be forthcoming only if more collaborative relationships are developed.

In addition to the difficulty of limited resources, the opportunities for cooperative problem solving are limited by ideological conflicts and limitations imposed by the requirements of an institution's objectives. An example of the latter occurs when one or more faculty must be dismissed and replaced if a department is to improve its competence. Sometimes it is possible to find alternatives other than firing or retaining the person in his initial role, but the realities are not always so kind.

Of all the blocks to collaborative governance, however, the ideological confrontation is the most critical on some campuses. It is paralyzing in itself, and it also may evoke legislative or trustee intervention to restrict the options for action. In the Berkeley confrontation between the Free Speech Movement and the University's chancellor, it became apparent that some of the FSM leaders had a primary interest not in consensus on the immediate issues, but in alteration of the system of university governance itself. They called for "an overthrow of the establishment." Sometimes the options are limited in a similar way by a rigid stance on prerogative on the part of some of the parties to the dispute. For example, on a number of campuses visited by the Task Force on Faculty Representation, the campus president took such a view of his authority and acceded to, say, the creation of a senate only if he could use subtler devices for having his own way.

There are, then, genuine limits to the possibility of avoiding on-campus clashes of will that end in a division of resources and opportunity on a win-or-lose basis. It does not follow that if one party refuses to cooperate, everyone else should also adopt the same strategy; but sometimes they should. On one campus, for example, the president refused to share authority in budget and faculty appointments, prevented faculty from reaching the trustees with their concerns, and had the support of the public in denying effective voice to the faculty. The faculty employed a strike to coerce him to share authority. Their doing so to gain a role appropriate to their competences, potential contributions, and rights as professionals is distinguishable from their seeking to take over authority which the president should retain. The spirit of collaboration which respects the rights and contributions of the different parties is not to be confused with weakness, timidity, or inability to uphold participants' rights. A frank facing of the attitudes of disputing parties about sharing authority may be an essential step in making the sharing genuine.

Sometimes when a constituent group refuses to collaborate, the most effective first step available is a reconsideration of its own position by the administration. The administrative position may have been based upon a false estimate of the importance of one of the issues or a false view of the depth of feeling and level of priority which the issue had for the constituents. On one campus, Negro students demanded massive funds, curricular autonomy, and dismissal of a white administrator of their program. The change of administrators was already viewed by the president as essential, though he had not made his view known because no replacement had been identified and no way had been found to avoid embarrassment of a faithful and previously effective staff member. When, however, in response to confrontation, the president acknowledged the merits of the demand for a change of program head and removed him, the other issues were settled on mutually acceptable criteria. In such a case the "establishment" itself had failed to let rationality rule and had thereby, albeit passively, provoked the constituents to use irrational means.

Even if a campus' constituencies desire to work together productively with a new sharing of prerogatives, it will not be easy to do so. It is inherent in the requirements of an effective institution of higher learning that cooperation within it be difficult. Its work creates controversy about what is true, what is good, which of the true and good things are most urgent, and who can do them best and how. Normally, the extent of trust and the diversity of attitudes and objectives bearing upon collaboration are a very mixed bag: the practical question in sharing authority is one as to the dominant climate and the working possibilities.

Trust as here discussed is also difficult to develop and sustain, for it is not a matter of expecting agreement or expecting others to act always in one's own interests. It is not even an assurance that the other parties will do what they say. It *is* a matter of reasonable predictability, of respect for the other party's purpose and intent, and of understanding the basis for his acts, even when they oppose one's own concerns. While it furthers predictability if one can count on what others say, we can know one another well enough to know when to take a statement as a basis for prediction and when not. Realism about the limits of agreement and consent can foster effective cooperation in a context of only partially shared objectives. This realism is better for collaboration than a sentiment for cooperation which misreads the obstacles to its effectuation.

In the face of all of these obstacles, the crucial resource of a campus for a strategy of collaboration in sharing authority is the respect for other individuals and cultures which is inherent in the commitment to inquiry. When respect for another individual or group includes respect for his values and priorities, as discussed in the preceding subsection on communication of "feeling," even the necessity of dividing inadequate resources cannot destroy a climate of creative sharing. It is equally important, however, that study and debate lead to the revision of judgments of fact and value by the disclosure of better analysis, more data, and better reasons than were previously available. As one of our consultants pointed out, this use of intelligence to adjudicate conflicts, redefine and transform interests and preferences, and revise goals is at the heart of the idea that consent should be rooted in reasoned discussion. The annual budget-making process is not only an occasion for cutting commitments to fit resources, but also one for clarification of priorities and the reasons for them. The councils and committees of a campus, too, must rule for one rather than another course of action from time to time; but their function is best served when they also bring the skills of cooperative inquiry to bear upon the clarification of the intellectual capabilities and services of the campus.

Even with the best of strategies for the achievement of consent, campuses are still likely to experience impasses as constituents demand and obtain voice. As with the strike by faculty, the veto of funds by legislators, or the boycott by students, campus leaders will be obliged to cope with impasses in ways that keep open the possibility of a future return to the strategies of collaboration.

ACCOUNTING TO THE CONSENTERS

The sharing of power is not fully effective unless a regular accounting is rendered in respect to the decisions made and the responsibilities delegated. If the accounting discloses unacceptable achievement or failure on the agreed-upon actions, the consenters should either alter the terms of agreements or change management. Even with satisfactory performance on objectives, the consenters may use the occasion of accounting to reconsider and alter their agreements, and perhaps to change elements of the management. Midcourse corrections should be expected as an aid to improving performance.

With this general principle of accountability, we have no quarrel. In observations of campus practice, however, we have discovered a number of characteristics of good account rendering that are often violated. We set down here some of these characteristics and examples of mechanisms whose wider use would improve practice.

An adequate process of accounting and assessing should have the following characteristics: precise articulation of accounting rendered to the responsibilities delegated; regularity and timing of accounting to permit timely reconsideration of agreements and arrangements; audits credible to those to whom account is being rendered; and adequacy of the accounting to its intended function.

Articulation of Assessment with Objectives

If a professor is expected to be a good teacher, a report on the quality of his research is obviously not adequately articulated with his responsibility to be a good teacher. There is presumably a relationship, but an audit of his work should not leave the connection to needless speculation. If a college is set up to elicit learning and maturity among its students, the audit should report on their learning and maturity—not on their ability scores, income after graduation, Woodrow Wilson Fellowships won; not on the financial assets of the college; and not even on the proportion of students getting doctorates or on learning outcomes other than those sought unless these data can be better related to the objectives than other evidences that could have been obtained. Far too many campus administrators use the excuse of having no appropriate measure for reporting on the wrong things. It would be better to get even unreliable data on the right thing than the most reliable data on the wrong objectives.

Regularity and Timeliness of Audit

In financial reporting it is common practice today to have annual reports of past and projected outcomes on the major financial objectives, quarterly or monthly reports that are useful in the finer control of the component operations of a campus, and daily or continuous accounting of operations that require continuous control. This feedback has to be selective in order to be usable for the objectives that have priority, and it has to be timed to permit changes in practice while they can still help to achieve the desired end results on different time periods.

Educational accounting is much chancier and more uncertain than financial accounting, but the characteristics of good processes of educational accounting are analogous. An educational innovation that is studied and reported upon only at the outset and at the end of a three-year period is unlikely to be well monitored for the purpose of enabling the educational policy and program council to improve its judgments. On the other hand, unlike a good set of thermostatic controls in a heating and air-conditioning system, continuous feedback on an educational innovation can in some forms seriously disturb the learning processes being monitored. (Unobtrusive measures can in some cases reveal what is going on without disturbing the processes being monitored.)

Credible Reporting

Where a campus' constituencies have sharply different cultural or educational frames of reference, or where they have problems of mutual trust, there may be great difficulty in obtaining feedback that is believed by those whose consent and decisions are needed. To meet this problem, it may be necessary not only to have agreement from the outset as to the types of data and the criteria on which feedback is wanted, but also to man the staff and boards with people who have the trust of the various constituencies. The modes of communication may also require tailoring to suit the requirements of the different constituencies. Informal communications may play a more important role in achieving understanding and agreement than formal occasions which give the final form and approval to a decision.

Many of the current reforms giving voice to students, faculty, and hitherto disfranchised groups on campus will have less effect than intended because they provide no practical process of feedback and accounting to the constituencies on the matters requiring their agreement and collaboration. No formula for this feedback and accounting will fit every campus. Yet changes in the makeup of governing structures to accommodate new constituencies should be accompanied at once by plans to inform their leaders and representatives as to the successes and failures of efforts to implement their decisions.

One of the problems of credibility encountered during the Campus Governance Program interviews had to do with the conflicting demands of confidentiality and credibility. A faculty member is dismissed or refused tenure. His advocates protest. The evidence is by policy not public. Unless the disputants can agree to submit the evidence to a trusted representative of the protesters or to a mutually trusted third party, with whom it stops, the disagreement remains unresolved. However, on some campuses secrecy was often maintained about types of information which were routinely available on other campuses. For example, on many public college campuses it is established policy that salary lists are open to the public; whereas on other campuses this information was not available even to elected representatives of faculty or students. Our interviews disclosed that such secrecy often sparked false rumors and prevented rebuttal with better authenticated facts.

A further problem of credibility arose around the question of the responsibility of those who know to inform those who do not know about the existence of information which the uninformed would view as important. Failure to inform in such cases was sometimes inadvertent and sometimes a matter of judgment about who ought to know. To sustain the confidence of its constituents, a campus needs to develop shared expectations about the responsibilities of seeking and providing information.

Adequacy of Accounting to Its Function

In addition to being timely, credible, and valid (articulated to its objective), the accounting of a campus to its constituents should ideally be intelligible to them, manageable in form, reliable, and sufficient to its functions. This is a hard prescription. Some campuses had a surfeit of feedback on some issues—more than the constituents could absorb, and sometimes too technical for them to understand. The communication channels can become so flooded with announcements, reports, and position papers that a constituent learns too late about the precise part of this flood that would have enabled him to pursue his interest with effect. Efforts to "computerize information feedback" have been known to "overload the circuits" rather than facilitate communication. Moreover, when the right information gets to the interested party, the time for digesting and using it may be inadequate. In other words, the cost of getting and using information can outweigh its utility or create an unmanageable problem for effective conduct of operations. How can the effort to share authority be prevented from diminishing the effectiveness of an organization for the purposes the sharers have in mind? Among the means are a continual focus upon aims and priorities in day-to-day decisions, use of varied means of communication, and care in keeping the governance and communication processes themselves under review.

To avoid a self-defeating burden of studies and reports, campus leaders are obliged to focus upon issues that most critically affect the bearing of day-to-day activities upon the campus' primary objectives. As a campus adds faculty or drops programs, replaces key officers, tries to set new admissions policies, decide on its proper size, establish new relationships with other institutions, or raise money, it will do well to think repeatedly about its aims—what students it wants to serve and how, what intellectual explorations it is particularly equipped to make, what ideas it would like to stand for. These aims are implemented, after all, in the "nuts-and-bolts" arrangements of daily institutional life.

As the tools and experience of communication develop, the variety of ways to render accounting increases. The means range from self-study to ongoing research on institutional functioning, from review committees or task groups to visiting consultants, from the use of annual budget conflicts in clarifying priorities to deciding how to design a proposal for foundation grants to be congruent with college purposes. Even the decisions of individuals about their own job definitions or the consultation of dean and department chairman with key faculty about their work may have an important effect in fostering coherent mustering of a campus' resources to implement consciously chosen objectives. Indeed, many campuses may want to develop their own yardsticks for assessment where local conditions or objectives differ from those of other campuses. Moreover, the development of its own assessment procedures can disclose much about the real objectives of an institution.

In these and other ways, the question of a campus' mission and style can be kept before the consenting constituencies and kept relevant to their decisions. A clearly articulated consensus will by no means emerge easily or remain comfortably intact. A critical element of a program to keep the level of working agreement on a campus effective is attention in the communication processes to the system of governance and communications itself. A number of tools have recently become available to help on this score.

A number of research questionnaires, though developed for purposes of research comparing numbers of campuses, can be used to help work out improvements of governance on a specific campus. Among these are the Pre-Interview Questionnaire of the Campus Governance Program; the College Trustee Survey, also of CGP; the Institutional Functioning Inventory; the Survey of College Goals and Objectives; and the Activities Index and College Characteristics Index (taken together to give a need–press profile as illustrated earlier in Chapter 2).

A number of precautions should be taken in the use of these tools. These precautions can be put as questions.

First, who should have the data? Much institutional research is wasted because the data are first reported to someone like the president or a dean, who may be too busy to decide whether to pass the data along or who may decide that some of it is too delicate to risk releasing the report at all. Data have also been worse than wasted when reported without adequate interpretation to people unaware of the hazards of interpretation (this has occurred with aptitude scores, for example).

When asked to provide consulting that used insights from the Campus Governance Program, some staff have taken the view that they would use the Pre-Interview Questionnaire (a survey of perceived campus problem areas and nominations of informed and influential people) only if they could report directly to the various constituencies of a campus (students, faculty, trustees, administrators, etc.). The consultants thus defined themselves as accountable to those constituencies. Normally, different parts of the data strike different constituencies as crucial. It is also common that feedback of data from the PIQ evokes supplemental interpretation from different constituencies and sometimes evokes conflict as to the meaning and significance of recent events. If it is then possible to have the different constituencies share and talk out these conflicting and complementary interpretations, it is also sometimes possible to devise or discover fruitful resolutions of specific problems or fruitful changes in management or governance. These changes might otherwise have been delayed or never made. On the basis of this experience as well as upon the general principle earlier enunciated regarding the sharing of authority and responsibility, the Campus Governance Program has sought to increase the feedback of research data to diverse campus constituencies. On some campuses it would be well to reduce the studies made in order to increase the dissemination of and deliberation upon the ones that are done.

A second precaution is suggested by the question: Who should interpret the data? Obviously, research data call for the help of professionals who know about the difficulties of sampling, reliability, validity, factor analysis, naming of scales, inferences that are legitimate under the circumstances of study, etc. At the same time, no campus constituency should allow itself to be the captive of a single professional researcher's point of view in the selection of what is significant and in hypothesizing about the relevance of this selection of materials for his own or another campus. A consultant or an intelligent layman with a modest background in research methods can provide helpful counterinterpretations and selections of data.

Third, whose point of view should govern the choice of questions, questioners, and framework for the appraisal of what is good or bad in current practices and problems? Researchers, as we have said already, are not neutral. Their very questions—and questionnaires—are selective (reflecting opinions and convictions about what it is important to ask) and value-laden (even "descriptive nouns" reflect decisions about what in a situation deserves attention or best sets the framework for definition of problems). It is not possible to avoid the results of selection in our efforts to analyze and study, but one can notice whose selection is initially at work and ask whether other selections of emphasis would helpfully correct or complement the initial one.

A related question is, Who should choose a campus' consultants? In choosing a psychiatrist one chooses the kind of advice he will get. So too with consultants on governance. The president of a distinguished private college recently acceded to student demands for outside perspective on the management and governance of that campus, but *he* appointed the consultant. Clearly he was still in full control.

When the Congress wishes to monitor the work of the President of the United States, it does not ask the President to name the investigating committee. While a campus is not the nation, and normally ought not to view its governance as an encounter of political adversaries, it should see that the perspectives governing its self-study give promise of implementing its intended mode of sharing authority.

A fourth precaution turns on the question: To what extent is self-help in the reformation of a campus' governance feasible and desirable? Self-help is always a matter of degree, and capability for self-help should be continuously cultivated. It is often best cultivated by arrangements in which it is exercised; but where some dependency is essential to effectiveness, then there should be diminishing dependency upon external authority. In consulting on governance, for example, some Campus Governance Program staff have favored arrangements in which an external team of faculty, students, and administrators was complemented by an internal campus team of similar composition. The on-campus team helped to plan the visit, took part in the daily planning of the next day's work, and participated in ways that equipped it to carry on the work and to help with similar work elsewhere.

This type of procedure has a number of advantages. It increases the capability of the constituencies on a campus to choose the next questions, questioners, and frames of reference for self-study. It spreads the awareness of data and the acceptance of responsibility for their use. A larger number of people of more diverse constituencies than would otherwise be possible become familiar with the possibilities and limitations of such work. In short, at one and the same time it ensures the sponsorship congruent with shared authority and increases the competence for later self-study. It also normally contributes to the credibility of the findings among the diverse constituencies of the campus.

A fifth precaution should finally be mentioned: How can a campus increase the chances that inquiry into its governance will get at the keys to needed change? Too often self-studies merely gloss over the deepest sores and allow the root problems to persist without treatment. How many consultants have been asked for help only to discover that the problem was "too delicate" to face. Probing questions about governance are often about as welcome as similar questions about sex life were some quarter of a century ago. They meet with a similar sense of shock and offense about invasion of privacy. It is true that individual dignity and privacy deserve respect. It is also true that the governing and managing of a college, private or public, is a public trust. The public interest is too vitally affected to justify silence or inaction because of the potential embarrassment of people who fail to serve the public interest.

Our discussion of accountability thus brings us back again to the basic reason for realignment of authority in campus governance: it is essential to fulfillment of the public trust embedded in the chartering of colleges and universities.

LEADERSHIP FOR EFFECTIVENESS AND CONSENT

Very little of the work of a college or university can be done unless the students, professors, and other staff wish to do it. Some of the violence experienced on campuses is an ultimate resort in the denial of legitimacy for both the leadership and the institution. A penultimate resort, much more widespread, is the non-violent withholding of consent, as when students refuse to study or simply go through the motions without their hearts and minds engaged.

Without vigorous and competent leaders, on the other hand, a campus never attains distinction or else cannot sustain it for long. Governance and management based upon the consent of diverse constituencies call for leaders who can envisage a gain of effectiveness by way of the dispersion of authority and power. Three characteristics of a campus with such leaders are as follows: (a) its leaders have the confidence of their principal constituencies; (b) its administrators can work effectively with other leaders who differ sharply from them in priorities, background, ways of working, and types of effectiveness; and (c) its administrative leaders give priority to overall institutional effectiveness and carry out their consulting and managing in ways that serve the major needs of the different constituencies.

Legitimation of Leaders by Constituencies

Reference was made earlier (page 101) to Dahl's explanation of the reliability, durability, efficiency, and effectiveness of legitimated leadership. A leader has "legitimacy" if his decisions are accepted not solely from fear of negative sanctions or coercion, but also from a belief in the rightness of the governing structure and leadership. The need for such leaders and the fact that influence is unevenly distributed does not imply that there is a ruling elite. Nor does the efficiency of legitimated leadership imply that participatory democracy is the most efficient form of government.[5]

Interview data on five presidents' patterns of consulting and delegating authority illustrate the complexity of relationships between legitimation and effectiveness.[6] The first president was an autocrat who had broad constituency support during a period of commonly acknowledged need for vigorous action. "The President is like a father to us in a good way," said one faculty member. "The present governance," another stated, "is a benevolent dictatorship for modernization." "Our president," reported a third interviewee, "has been the driving force . . . . He is authoritarian and has to be." He pressed an academic senate into existence to get a responsible faculty body with which he could consult effectively. "He has tremendous capability," said a faculty member about his relations with the senate. "They come away thinking they did it themselves, and they did; but he set the framework." "Most people feel that they are in a productive setting." Another faculty or student body might be disturbed by the president's setting the framework, but on this campus his style was welcome and productive. The retiring president of University B, sketched in Chapter 2, had a more ambivalent acceptance but had sustained his legitimation until his term ended.

The president of another campus, no more autocratic, failed to get the acceptance achieved by the first. His consulting was less systematic, more secretive, less supportive of those to whom he had delegated authority. "The president informally consults with

---

[5] Dahl, *op. cit.*, pp. 16-17.

[6] These and other interview data on the presidents are reported by Hodgkinson, 54.

(a certain faculty member) about just about everything, although people rarely know this. Also with (a certain administrator); if a decision is made and (that administrator) doesn't like it, then the decision won't get made." With others, however, people were "going around end." "Since the dean has to go to the president, it's a shorter cut to go to the president directly." This style affected communications. "Only time I know a person's hired is when he shows up," one department chairman remarked. Many interviews on this campus reported a highly organized rumor mill alongside an ineffective formal system of communication.

The president of a fourth campus deliberately turned away from the type of administration represented in the preceding three examples. He rapidly thrust responsibilities upon others who, in both their own and others' eyes, had less competence and less capacity for initiative than was needed. They could not tolerate the resulting ambiguity: "The structure needs more specific job descriptions, more designation of responsibilities. No one follows through; the system has been established, but it doesn't result in action. Problems are recognized, but sometimes everyone's responsibility becomes no one's responsibility." "There is a wonderful dependence of the president upon his subordinates, but these persons are inexperienced." A number of the staff themselves saw the president as not holding them adequately accountable for their decisions.

A fifth president, as active a decentralizer as the fourth, suffered problems, but with better effect. "I have delegated out of my office responsibilities for the daily workings . . . . All decisions, or almost all, are made before they reach me . . . . Decentralization . . . has resulted in conflict at lower levels. If it persists, I resolve it eventually. We feel free to move around; tend not to be bound by channels and communication pathways." This president, like the first cited above, had worked hard to get a faculty senate; but he wanted it to make decisions even if different than what he would have made and even if outside the prior boundaries he had suggested. He wanted students in the senate and on all other campus committees. As in the fourth campus just cited, many felt unready for the president's speed in sharing authority. "The administration is very much interested in having students make academic decisions. In the past two years we have had some people interested in student government, but they can't get anything done. The things that go on in Student Senate are forensic and not relevant." "In the Faculty

Senate," said another person, "there is some responsiveness. We have a great deal of freedom and are just beginning to exercise it." Some faculty and students were fearful of the power being given to faculty : "The Faculty Senate is becoming more powerful, the president less . . . I see this as a dangerous thing." This president, however, had also introduced practices in support of those newly in authority, provided structures for accountability, and had managed to create a climate of growing effectiveness along with the awareness of problems.

A president's effectiveness depends upon his continuing enjoyment of legitimation by his various constituencies. Douglas M. Knight, former president of Lawrence University and later of Duke University, commented on this point:

> In some ways the university president has always been a political figure with several constituencies . . . once he has been chosen for (office), he finds himself responsible not just to the party which has elected him, but to every party which thinks it has a legitimate interest in the affairs of the institution. The number of those parties has grown in recent years . . . .

> But nobody in his right mind could claim that these groups are very often in easy agreement with one another.[7]

A president has the responsibility, for the good of the institution, to elicit a workable partnership among these constituencies; but he does not have the power to make them agree. Knight contends that for the president's task to be viable, there must be "a restructuring of the whole idea of university government, so that those who have both authority and true power in various areas take the responsibility that goes along with their power.[8]

A similar relationship between legitimation and constituencies' consent appears in other leadership roles. In their responses to the Pre-Interview Questionnaire, department chairmen characteristically shared more faculty concerns than did other administrators, shared more student concerns than did other faculty, and shared more of the concerns of other administrators

---

[7] *Trustee* 24 : 1; June 1970 (Division of Higher Education in the United Methodist Church, PO Box 871, Nashville, Tenn. 37202).

[8] *Ibid.*, p. 2.

than did either students or other faculty.[9] Common sense suggests that this finding is to be expected because department chairmen must listen to, and mediate among, these groups day by day. Apparently success in the chairman role is in part a matter of the ability of the chairman to accommodate the concerns of the various groups to one another and to facilitate a degree of achievement of each group's concerns which is satisfactory or tolerable to it. If a president or a department chairman cannot elicit such a working relationship, there is a crisis of confidence. Someone must back down or withdraw or be replaced, or the institution must lose effectiveness or even be dissolved. On one campus in our study the president invoked state authority and police power to put down opposition in such a crisis. On another the president acceded to militant student and community pressures and persuaded the faculty to go along, but the president resigned shortly thereafter.

One of the complications in present-day campus leadership is that the list of acknowledged constituencies and their makeup undergo rapid change. A leader who had a mandate, as Dr. Knight stated, might find it out of date in its practicability. For example, a few departments in the Nineteen Campus Study were beginning to define the department as including not only faculty, but also the students majoring in the department, and in rare cases the nonmajors using departmental services. In a sense, this new element had been represented all along through the responsiveness of the chairman and the faculty to student concerns. The change was in a new expectation by students, viewed as a right, that they be asked for advice before decisions and in at least one case be permitted to elect representatives to take part in department meetings.

It is not a new story that a leader may lose the following with which he began or that constituencies may change their concerns and their response to a leader after he has held office for a period of time. There does seem to be something new in the rapidity and frequency of such changes and in the likelihood that new claimants to a voice will emerge who can indeed force consideration of their claims. This condition, in turn, calls for provision in the very design of campus governance itself that such claims be considered and settled in ways that take account

---

[9] Metty, 72.

of the merits of the conflicting views and yield new effectiveness in the institution.

Working with Many Leaders

One important vehicle for voicing and settling changing constituents' concerns is the presence of active leaders among them. Leadership is not to be confused with management. Leadership without good management is ineffective. Good management without good leadership gets the wrong things or irrelevant things done. The two are essential partners, but they are not one and the same.

Campuses generally function best if the president and some other key administrators are good leaders as well as good managers. But where they are, a lopsidedness is likely to develop in the representation of diverse campus constituencies unless these constituencies also have effective leadership. These constituency leaders should also be good managers, but for different reasons. Their task is to see that the accounting due their constituencies is well done by those who render it and that their constituencies' interests, perspectives, and purposes are well served in the institution. Ideally, they will see that their constituencies are educated in the advantages, implications, requirements, and consequences of collaboration in governance. When other constituencies refuse to play this game, the constituency leaders will face the task of upholding their group's concerns and perspectives while trying to rectify the basis for collaboration.

Leadership is also not to be confused with being a representative on councils, boards, and committees. Being elected does not make one a leader. Being elected or being an appointed representative also does not guarantee that one knows or effectively embodies the perspectives and concerns of his constituency. As elections are often arranged, it is also not possible to know who a given representative has for a constituency. There is much disagreement and confusion as to whether an elected representative should act as an instructed delegate or should exercise a leadership role in ways that go beyond his constituents' readiness or understanding. Finally, a leader, as Dahl pointed out, is one who actually enjoys influence among his constituency. Those who get elected do so often for causes other than enjoying influence and, even when elected on this basis, often lose it.

There is increasing awareness today among both students and faculty about these distinctions. Realism, sometimes called cynicism, is increasing about the claims of peers to represent the perspectives, priorities, and perceptions of their group. Peer "leaders" themselves may lack credibility or legitimation. One of the disclosures of our data on where to get information and who can get things done (see Chapter 2, Highlight 9) is that students and faculty rarely nominate their own members first for these capabilities in reference to their priority concerns. The implication is that a vacuum of leadership exists among them. If administrators control both information and its use, what power can peer leaders have?

When a campus faculty, student body, or other grouping is essentially leaderless, how can leaders be assisted to emerge without being reputedly or actually captive of those already in power? How can inexperienced constituency leaders gain the training and support they need without being so co-opted by the campus administration that their effectiveness and influence are diminished? Our interviews showed these needs in regard to constituents' leadership but contained few clues as to how to meet them. The Task Force on Faculty Representation insisted strongly that administratively appointed faculty on academic senates and other governing bodies were no substitute for faculty chosen leadership. The same point seems to apply to student or outside community representation. One factor that seems to have encouraged emergence of such leaders is restraint on the part of the administration: refraining from creating its own set of chosen consultants or officeholders, patience in waiting for the leaders to emerge, acceptance of the constituents' own views of the kinds of competence they wanted in their spokesmen, and willingness to put resources at the command of such leaders when they emerged.

Focus upon Institutional Effectiveness

Implicit in the leaders' continuing legitimation by changing constituencies is their confidence in the leaders' priorities and the possibility of continuous changes in the concept of institutional effectiveness. If those enfranchised are to include faculty, students, administrators, nonfaculty staff, and trustees, and if the trustees in turn include the alumni, parents of students, church authorities, or other elements of the public, how can the leaders maintain a clear and stable enough vision of effectiveness to do their work? The processes and structures for developing and maintaining consent, which were discussed in the first section of this chapter, can also serve to keep the concept of effectiveness under review. There are, however, special difficulties with issues of purpose and priority which affect the concept of effectiveness. They often involve the consent of trustees or others who are nonresidents and whose participation is thus more limited and more difficult to arrange than for residents. Issues of institutional purpose and priorities have a scope and importance which may make them more difficult to negotiate when disagreement among constituents is fundamental. The abstractness of issues of purpose and priority also makes it difficult to reach operationally clear agreements or to render accounting to the satisfaction of constituents.

The effectiveness and productivity which concern the campus' constituencies are matters of impact in relation to various purposes and functions approved by these constituencies. This concept of institutional effectiveness is difficult to apply as well as to state. Easier concepts come readily to mind: participant satisfaction, minimization of disorder, cost per student per period of time, growth in size and assets of the institution, and so on. Early in our study we were urged to use such criteria: at least they would tell us something definite, we were advised. But these criteria do not express what any of the major constituencies want a college or university to be and do. At best they get at only part of what interests the constituencies.

To see the full complexity of the criterion of effectiveness, we must also note that the concern for good governance is not merely one of effectiveness in achieving the impact desired, but one of gaining that impact at relatively advantageous cost in the face of limited resources and often peculiar circumstances. To find a way to assess relative cost/benefit ratios in these terms is at present a task on which only the crudest of successes is possible.

A final complication in the criterion of effectiveness results from the fact that the voice which constituents—students, nonfaculty staff, faculty, alumni, and others—have in governance is itself a factor in creating the impact desired. The role of students in governance, for example, may contribute to the learning and maturing which is a campus goal for students, or that role may be exercised in a way that has adverse effects upon learning and maturing. Whichever way students participate, there will be costs and benefits in their doing so. Under some forms of participation, the costs are offset by high yields in learning and maturing. Moreover, while current participant satisfaction is not itself a primary goal in the eyes of most campus constituencies, it is usually an objective of college life to make learning and democratic association attractive and rewarding. Doing so is essential to the future of an intellectual, democratic society. (Today the very meaning and morality of being democratic are issues on some campuses; on these campuses the attractiveness and reward of a democratic community depend not simply upon its personal satisfactions, but more profoundly upon its compatibility with a just relation to one's fellowmen.) These thoughts imply that it is not simply immediate yield of learning in relation to costs that should be a campus goal, but long-range benefit at reasonable cost.

These difficulties with understanding and achieving the effectiveness requisite to confidence in a campus' leaders affect their task profoundly. Much of the work of "hearing and heeding" the constituencies must be done by way of day-to-day administrative processes. It will not do to rely wholly upon constituents' access to policy-making councils and committees for their influence. Interviewers in the Nineteen Campus Study reported numerous examples of administrative practice which were viewed as hindering or contributing to the constituents' sense that their concerns were receiving due hearing. The examples are used here to state hypotheses about the characteristics of effective administrative leadership. In view of the ever-present limitations of time and resources relative to the problems and opportunities for administrative effort, the list is one on which only partial success is possible.

Stress on keeping institutional goals attuned to changing needs and on keeping practice congruent with the avowed goals. On two campuses, as mentioned before, the readiness of students for intellectual demands had increased significantly over a period of years. The demands placed upon them, as reported by students, had not changed significantly. Although teaching that provided strong intellectual stimulus was an important priority on each campus, there was no regular means for obtaining or considering the appropriate response to this type of data. One of these two institutions, however, had been very active in surveying statewide supply and demand for graduate studies and was adapting rapidly to the opportunity to expand its graduate programs. A major effort was under way to enlist faculty and students in assessing the priorities for graduate programs.

Subordination of established procedures and policy details to the goals and objectives established in those policies and in the institution's mandate. On one campus interviewees claimed that the office of dean of students was a repository for styles that adults would like students to practice, but that most students did not believe in or practice.[10] On most campuses there were issues about one or more regulations about dormitory life or student conduct which students claimed were incompatible with the objectives of either social or academic policy. In one case a staff respondent charged an administrator with explicitly countermanding institutional policy: "In several cases of interracial dating, the dean of women has called the girls in and taken two stands: (a) paternalistic warning of the dangers involved, and (b) paternalistic disapproval." Another common complaint had to do with procedures in budgeting and finance which had the effect of nullifying or altering educational priorities.

Support by one constituency's leaders (or one function's managers) of the needs and rights of other constituencies and their leaders. A frequent limitation reported by or about deans of students was the failure of faculty support. Some incumbents may not have deserved the support, but its absence reduced effectiveness in any event. On a number of campuses the dean of students was viewed among faculty and students as essentially a student advocate; on one campus this emphasis was embedded in policy and had general support; in other cases the faculty were not united on the issue. The dean, a sample comment went, "is too directly involved with students." "People in (that) office are too approachable for their own effectiveness." On one campus numerous faculty reported that the business manager made academic decisions by selective denial of funds: "Hell of a time with the business manager . . . arbitrary . . . going into areas and making arbitrary decisions." "Business manager in some ways controls the academic program." Whatever the merits of these claims, the campuses lacked a sense of effective teamwork.

Support for delegation of authority and division of labor. The sketches of presidents' consulting styles have already illustrated this point. On the two campuses where the deans of students were most respected, the clarity of delegated authority and the predictability of the dean's performance were cited as causes. "He may give you a 'no' answer . . . but he gives you an answer." "We have confidence in (the dean) ; no need to go to the president

---

[10] Hodgkinson reports our interview data in three papers on deans of students and business managers (44, 46, 47).

to fight battles." "Outside of the president's office the person who solves his own problems is (the dean of students)." By contrast, it was said of a poorly functioning dean's office: "The president has encouraged students to deal directly with the central administration . . . . (He) was not relying on the counsel of the dean of students."

Openness and reliability in communications. Of a respected dean, one informant said: "Next to the president I would go to him for information. He knows a great deal, and always respects confidentiality of student information." "This office tries to sound out as many people as are going to be affected by the decisions which it makes." On one campus, on the other hand, some major administrators were criticized for "overwhelming the critics with superior information."

Subordination of the needs of a particular job or office to those of the institution or of a more inclusive task or division. Some administrators were perceived as preoccupied with their own advancement or with the power of their departments or offices.

In summary, those presidents and other leaders seemed to have the greatest convergence of energy upon task where their constituents stressed the sense of having their concerns respected, of being important members of the team effort, of being able effectively to get their observations and interests heard and heeded, and of sharing on their own terms in any gains that were being made through the institution's efforts. In these situations the institution's leadership enjoyed prerogatives and resources for coercion but relied primarily upon the perceived rightness of their priorities, their insight into the institution's requirements, and effectiveness in meeting these priority concerns.

Summary of Recommendations

The recommendations of this book bear upon two questions: Who should share authority on campus? How can the sharing of authority be made effective?

WHO SHOULD GOVERN?

> A. Who should share the authority? Most campuses should make substantial changes toward more effective enfranchisement of faculty, students, nonfaculty staff, and underrepresented elements of the public. The administrators and these groups are here called the constituencies of the campus.

> B. Why share authority among these constituencies? Four claims to authority must be heeded if a college or university is to do its best work. The claims apply differently to each constituency. They must be reconciled in the choice of purpose, priorities, and programs of the campus. The four types of claims are:

> 1. Concerns that are critically affected by the work of the campus

146

    2. Competences essential to the work of the campus

    3. Need for cooperation of the constituency

    4. Rights of sponsors and providers of resources.

The current crisis in campus governance is primarily one of doubt and disagreement about the satisfaction of these claims in the choice of purposes, style, and priorities. The fuller enfranchisement of constituencies must be used to transform the climate of doubt and disagreement, where it prevails, into one of effective collaboration.

C. What criteria should govern the realignment of authority on campus? The tasks and trends confronting higher education do not dictate any one style of governing that will serve all campuses. They do suggest criteria for the patterns of governance that are likely to be effective:

1. The authority structure should reflect a genuine commitment to enfranchise constituencies previously unrepresented or underrepresented. This principle does not imply direct participation of particular constituents in the board of trustees, but it does require arrangements which provide for effective advocacy of, and response to, their concerns.

2. The processes and prerogatives in governing should be so designed as to foster the cooperation of each constituency and to further the contributions for which it has special competence. At the same time the pattern of sharing authority should avoid undue influence of the special interests and disadvantages which the different constituencies bring with their roles.

3. The system of governance of a campus should provide for a division of labor between policy making and managing, and between the board of trustees and other councils and committees. The system should provide effective means for constituencies to be heard and heeded at the level and locus where their particular concerns receive final disposition. In state systems and in private institutions with multiple campuses this principle calls for mechanisms for these campuses and their constituencies to be heard at the statewide or systemwide level.

4. The existence of diverse constituencies with often conflicting interests and perspectives need not imply that all
fundamental policy making should become a process of
group negotiation—of collective bargaining, compromise,
and accommodation. At the same time, not every issue
will be settled on rationally persuasive grounds in the
eyes of every constituency. To reduce the frequency of
impasse and to minimize damage from it, the system of
government should provide mechanisms of accommodation short of coercion and violence. The enfranchisement
recommended in the first criterion should result in purposes and priorities which reflect constituency concerns
and minimize the likelihood of coercive confrontations.

5. The rapidity of external and internal changes affecting campuses requires processes of governance which are
more flexible in everyday operation, capable of more
rapid and effective response to crises, and less cumbersome to change in response to new working agreements
than have been typical in the past.

The implementation of these principles will affect substantially
the concepts and practices of a campus with regard to its specific
methods of governing and managing.

HOW CAN THE SHARING OF AUTHORITY BE EFFECTIVE?

Sharing authority can take two basic forms: deciding some things
jointly, and dividing the labor on others. Every campus has
a different governance problem from every other campus. But
some ways of sharing authority can contribute generally to effectiveness. This list can be used to evaluate current practices.

A. In dividing the labor, create units of government capable
of coherent purpose and high morale. For these units,
define the boundaries of their autonomy clearly and insist
upon accountability from those who lead and govern the
units.

B. At each level of operation (overall institution with the
trustees and president, colleges or institutes or divisions
or departments, etc.) work for the advantages of division
of labor. This division of labor takes many forms: be-

tween things decided jointly and things left to subgroups or individuals to decide, between policy making and managing, between things decided in advance and things decided after operations are under way, between loci (committees, offices, etc.) at which different types of issues or tasks are decided or managed, and between aspects of a task in which one group or another is accorded a predominant or distinctive voice, etc.

C. Know the specific facts as to how your own campus' constituencies view the problems, priorities, possibilities, and environment. This knowledge is generally missing or inadequate on today's campuses. Chapter 2 illustrates the ways it can bear upon the choice of purposes and methods on particular campuses.

D. Improve the mechanisms of representative government but put increasing reliance upon other ways of getting and maintaining constituents' consent and support: e.g., upon communications before decision and during operations, on informal but systematic and open consultation, and on scientific gathering of information on both concerns and performance.

E. Enforce the sharing of authority. Lip service to democratic practice will not do. Whether an administrator, a legislature, the trustees, or a violent minority seeks to defeat a genuine sharing of authority, the effort must be firmly resisted. No simple means of doing this are offered here. Astute and persistent firmness in making the principle work is what is needed.

F. Sharing authority is ideally a matter of each person respecting the concerns of the others as part of his own concerns. Where ideology or conflict of interests is too deep for this kind of collaboration, cooperation can be organized around mutual self-interest of people with different concerns. It should be a last resort that constituents of a campus fight out a division of resources and opportunity in which the gain of one is the loss of the other. Campus leaders should work to minimize this last way of sharing and to maximize the first two.

G. Not every issue can be settled on grounds that are rationally persuasive to every party. For such issues the system of governing should provide ways to decide and act short of violence. Some matters, even on a campus used to deciding things jointly by "reason," can best be settled by negotiation and bargaining. The enfranchisement of students, faculty, and other constituencies should result in purposes and priorities which minimize coercive confrontations.

H. Design governance to get decisions or action more rapidly than in the past, to be more flexible in applying purposes and priorities to changed circumstances and distinctive cases than in the past, and to permit revision of purposes and priorities in response to constituency concerns more readily than in the past. This principle is essential because of the basic and rapid change occurring in human society today.

I. Invest effort and resources in overcoming the obstacles to effective sharing of authority. A more democratic pattern of governance will not be easier, less organized, or cheaper. On the contrary, it will require more research, more training of participants and leaders, and greater costs. Among the obstacles to be overcome are interfering attitudes, more time needed for the tasks of joint deciding and delegated authority, needed incentives for those most capable of helping, need for checks upon self-interest and parochial attitudes of different participant groups and individuals, costs of improved communications, and difficulties of getting communications that inform rather than confuse or overwhelm people.

J. Learn to deal with emotional talk and action to gain understanding and cooperation rather than to escalate conflict and destruction. This involves reading behind the feeling to the message hidden in it, helping the inarticulate to say what they mean, translating messages from one ideological or cultural language to another, getting help on implementation for those with good ideas or relevant concerns but without practical know-how, and enlisting general understanding of novel concerns and ideas for which no common language exists.

K. Improve the patterns of accountability on campus and between campus and the public. To do this requires:

1. Precise articulation of reporting to the responsibilities delegated and the objectives adopted;

2. Timing of the reporting to permit timely reconsideration of agreements and arrangements;

3. Choosing people and methods of accounting which will be credible to those to whom account is being rendered;

4. Providing reports that are intelligible to the constituents, reliable, and usable by them and the managers for their intended purposes.

L. Enlist and develop leaders capable of being effective through sharing and dispersion of authority and power. These leaders will be, not less, but more, given to initiative as to purpose, priority, and program than are leaders who rely principally upon less collaborative ways of governing and managing. In addition, they will

1. Cultivate and sustain the confidence of their principal constituencies;

2. Work effectively with other leaders who differ sharply from them in priorities, background, ways of working, and types of effectiveness;

3. Give priority to overall institutional effectiveness, delegate heavily to other leaders and managers who put similar priority upon effective component colleges or units contributing to overall campus quality, and conceive the desired effectiveness in terms that serve the major needs of the different constituencies;

4. Take responsibility for accomplishing the things recommended in the preceding points.

M. Finally, there is no simple recipe for governing a college or university campus. No one style or definition of purpose will do for all. None of the preceding, simplified summary should be read as prescribing such a style or doctrine. The governing of an American college or university is an increasingly complex task. Each campus must find its own best way of coping with its own unique problems of governance.

EPILOGUE

The campus is a public trust. Its function is primarily that of providing intellectual services. Things intellectual, however, cannot be separated or shut off from things social, emotional, and political. Learning or research is not soundly intellectual if it ignores or underplays important aspects of the life of the individual or of the society. The growing numbers of people and complexity of society, the continuing growth of knowledge and technological achievement, and the rapid rate of social change combine to give the intellectual functions a rising importance. Both the well-being of society and the quality of higher education depend upon an improved performance of these increasingly important intellectual functions. It is to make this achievement possible that we here recommend a substantial increase and sophistication in the sharing of authority on campus.

Appendix A.
List of Materials Produced by the Campus Governance Program

THE TASK GROUP ON FACULTY REPRESENTATION AND ACADEMIC NEGOTIATIONS

(Directed by Arnold R. Weber, University of Chicago)

†1. Weber, Arnold R., et al. *Faculty Participation in Academic Governance.* Washington, D. C.: American Association for Higher Education (hereafter AAHE), 1967.

Derivative Papers

2. Hickman, C. Addison. "Academic Negotiations." AAHE Summer Conference, July 3, 1967. (Mimeo.)

3. ———. "Academic Negotiations." *College and University Bulletin* 20: 2-4; October 1, 1967.

4. ———. "College Faculty Participation in Academic Governance." *NEA Journal* 56: 46-48; October 1967.

5. ———. "Faculty Participation in Academic Governance." *The Faculty and Academic Policy.* Proceedings of the Second Minnesota Intercollegiate Faculty Conference. Grand Rapids, Minn., March 1968. pp. 49-69.

6. ———. "Faculty Role in Governance." *Handbook of College and University Administration: Academia.* (Edited by Asa S.

---

† Available from the Association as of September 1970.

Knowles.) New York: McGraw-Hill Book Co., 1970. Sec. 6, pp. 85-103.

7. ———. "The Faculty Voice in Institutional Policy." *AGB Reports* 10: 17-26; January 1968.

8. ———. "The Tenure System as Viewed by a Faculty Member." Presented to the Eighteenth Annual Legislative Work Conference of the Southern Regional Education Board. Hot Springs, Ark., July 1969. 8 pp. Subsequently published under the same title in *The College Campus in 1969: The Faculty*. Proceedings of the Eighteenth SREB Legislative Work Conference. Southern Regional Education Board, 1969. pp. 30-33.

9. Livingston, John C. "Academic Senate Under Fire." *Agony and Promise: Current Issues in Higher Education, 1969*. (Edited by G. Kerry Smith.) Washington, D. C.: AAHE, 1969. pp. 161-72.

10. ———. "Collective Negotiations." *Handbook of College and University Administration: Academia*. (Edited by Asa S. Knowles.) New York: McGraw-Hill Book Co., 1970. Sec. 6, pp. 104-19.

11. ———. "Faculty and Administrative Roles in Decision Making." *Stress and Campus Response: Current Issues in Higher Education, 1968*. (Edited by G. Kerry Smith.) Washington, D. C.: AAHE, 1968. pp. 187-95.

*12. Oberer, Walter E. "Faculty Participation in Academic Decision Making: As to What Issues, by What Forms, Using What Means of Persuasion?" *Employment Relations in Higher Education*. Bloomington, Ind.: Phi Delta Kappa (Eighth and Union, Bloomington 47401).

13. Rehmus, Charles M.; Peterson, John; and Umbeck, Sharvy G. "Comments on 'Academic Negotiations.' " AAHE Summer Conference, July 3, 1967. (Mimeo.)

THE COLLEGE TRUSTEE STUDY

(Directed by Morton Rauh, with the support of Antioch College, the Sloan Foundation, and the Campus Governance Program of AAHE, with staffing and support of the Educational Testing Service, and with cosponsorship of the Association of College and University Governing Boards)

14. Hartnett, Rodney. *College and University Trustees*. Princeton, N. J.: Educational Testing Service, 1968.

15. Rauh, Morton A. "The Trustees of Higher Education." *AGB Reports* 2: 3-25; January 1969.

---

* Work using Campus Governance Program data, financial support, or stimulus, but developed primarily under other auspices.

16. ———. "The Trustees of Higher Education—Who They Are and What They Think." Progress Report of the Campus Governance Program, Twenty-Fourth National Conference on Higher Education. March 4, 1969. (Mimeo.)

17. ———. *The Trusteeship of Colleges and Universities.* New York: McGraw-Hill Book Co., 1969.

18. ———. "Putting the Trust in Trustees." *Antioch Notes* 46: No. 8; 1-7; May 1969.

19. ———. "The Token Trustee." *Antioch Notes* 48: 1-7; September 1970.

THE NINETEEN CAMPUS STUDY

(Directed by Stephen B. Plumer, Syracuse University and Antioch College)

20–
38. Churchill, Ruth. "Description of Campus Problems of Nineteen Campuses During November 1968 to January 1969, Based on Pre-Interview Questionnaire Data." Washington, D. C.: AAHE, Fall 1969. Variable length, 12 pp. upward. (Mimeo.) Eight campuses have given permission to release separate reports on their own data. Available from Morris Keeton, Antioch College, Columbia, Md. 21043, $1 per copy.

39. ———. "The Use of the Pre-Interview Questionnaire for Describing College Problems." Washington, D.C.: AAHE, December 1963. 20 pp. Available as with Items 20-38 at $1 per copy.

40. Hauser, David R. "Introduction: Toward a New University." *Soundings* 2: 120-27; Summer 1969 (Society for Religion in Higher Education, 400 Prospect St., New Haven, Conn.)

41. ———. "The Uses of the University Revisited: Can We Talk About an Academic Community?" Conference of the Society for Religion in Higher Education, August 1968. (Mimeo.)

42. Hodgkinson, Harold L. "The Campus Psychiatrist—His Institutional Batting Average." *Proceedings of the Conference of American Association for Adolescent Psychiatry.* (In press.)

43. ———. "Current Alternatives in Campus Governance." December 1968. (Mimeo.)

44. ———. "The Dean of Students and Business Manager as Campus Pressure Centers." 1968. (Mimeo.)

45. ———. "Finding the Levers—The Folkways and Mores of Campus Governance and How To Make Them Work." *Effective College Teaching.* Washington, D. C.: American Council on Education, 1970.

46. ———. "How Deans of Students Are Seen by Others—and Why." Conference for Deans of Students sponsored by CRDHE and NASPA, San Diego, Calif., June 18-21, 1969. Same paper at ACPA, 1970. (Mimeo.)

47. ———. "How Deans of Students See Themselves—And Others." *NASPA Journal;* July 1970.

48. ———. "Governance and Factions—Who Decides Who Decides?" *The Research Reporter* 3: 4-7; 1968 (Center for Research and Development in Higher Education, Berkeley, Calif.).

49. ———. "Governance and Relevance for Those Over Thirty." AAHE Summer Conference, Dallas, Tex., July 1, 1968. Published in shortened version in *Decision Making in Higher Education.* Washington, D. C.: AAHE, September 11, 1968.

50. ———. "The Next Decade of Campus Governance." Berkeley, Calif.: Carnegie Foundation for the Advancement of Teaching, 1969. (Mimeo.)

51. ———. "Notes on Role Conflict in Campus Governance." National Conference on Higher Education, AAHE, March 1970. (Mimeo.)

52. ———. "The President and Campus Governance: A Research Profile." Washington, D. C.: American Council on Education, President's Institute, June 1969.

53. ———. "The President and Leadership Styles—A Research Report." *Educational Record,* Summer 1970.

54. ———. "The Structure and Function of Decision-Making Organizations Involved in Campus Governance." 1970. (Mimeo.)

55. ———. "Students and an Intellectual Community." *Educational Record* 40: 398-406; Fall 1968.

56. ———. "Student Participation in Campus Governance." AERA Conference, Los Angeles, Calif., February 8, 1969.

57. ———. "Teachers, Games, and Roles." Annual Conference on Administration, Center for the Study of Education, University of Michigan, June 22, 1967. (Mimeo.)

58. ———. "Today's Students and Tomorrow's University." Prepared for St. John's University, January 24, 1968. (Mimeo.)

59. ———. "Walden U.—A Utopian Model." *Soundings,* Summer 1969. Also in *The Identity Crisis of Higher Education.* (Edited by H. Hodgkinson.) San Francisco: Jossey-Bass, 1970.

60. ———. "Who Decides Who Decides?" *Agony and Promise: Current Issues in Higher Education, 1969.* (Edited by G. Kerry Smith.) Washington, D. C.: AAHE, 1969.

61. Imes, Suzanne. *Disparate Perceptions of Campus Problems.* Summary of Findings on the Pre-Interview Questionnaire for Nineteen Campuses, January 1970. 297 pp. (Mimeo.)

62. Keeton, Morris T. "A Call to Leadership." *Struggle and Promise: A Future for Colleges.* New York: McGraw-Hill Book Co., 1969. Chapter VI. Also published as "Liberal Arts Colleges: A Call to Leadership." *Journal of Higher Education* 39: 361-75; October 1968.

63. ———. "The Disenfranchised on Campus." *Journal of Higher Education* 40: 421-29; July 1970. Also presented to Information Session A, Highlights and Hypotheses from the AAHE Campus Governance Program, Twenty-Fifth National Conference on Higher Education, Chicago, March 2, 1970.

64. ———. "Dissonance in College Governance." Presented at the Danforth Workshop on Liberal Arts Education, Summer 1969.

65. ———. "Priorities for the Reform of Universities." Presented at the State University of New York Conference of Academic Vice-Presidents, August 1969.

66. ———. "A Productive Voice for Students." *New Prospects for the Small Liberal Arts College.* New York: Teachers College Press, Columbia University, 1968.

67. ———, with remarks by Nancy Timmins. "The Role of the Student in Academic Governance." *Powers and Responsibilities in Academic Governance—1969.* Proceedings of the Third Annual Summer Seminar on Academic Administration, July 13-25, 1969. Austin, Tex.: Association of Texas Colleges and Universities.

68. ———. "Shared Authority in Campus Governance." Presented to the Pennsylvania Association of Junior Colleges, October 11, 1969. (Mimeo.)

†69. ———. *Shared Authority on Campus.* Washington, D. C.: AAHE, 1971.

70. ———. "The Achievement of Quality in Private College Operations." *Models and Mavericks: A Profile of Liberal Arts Colleges.* Prepared for the Carnegie Commission on Higher Education, 1971. Chapter V. (In press.)

71. Meisler, Richard. "How To Communicate With Students." Progress Report on AAHE Campus Governance Program, Twenty-Fourth National Conference on Higher Education, Chicago, March 4, 1969.

72. Metty, Michael P. "The Department Chairman and the Public Institution." Progress Report on AAHE Campus Governance Program, Twenty-Fourth National Conference on Higher Education, Chicago, March 4, 1969.

73. Plumer, Stephen B. "Campus Word Games." *College and University Journal* 8: 3-6; Winter 1969.

---

† Available from the Association as of January 1971.

74. ———. "Evaluation of Administrative Effectiveness." Twenty-Second National Conference on Higher Education, Chicago, March 7, 1967.

75. ———. "Preliminary Report of AAHE's Campus Governance Program, Exploring the Faculty Mystique (Public College Faculty)." Twenty-Fourth National Conference on Higher Education, Chicago, March 4, 1969.

76. ———. "Some Observations About Selected Aspects of American Higher Education Generated by the Campus Governance Program. Decision Making in Higher Education. Washington, D. C.: AAHE, September 11, 1968. (Shortened version of talk at July Conference.)

77. Stern, George G. "Campus Environments and Student Unrest." *Agony and Promise: Current Issues in Higher Education, 1969.* (Edited by G. Kerry Smith.) Washington, D. C.: AAHE, 1969. pp. 123-38.

78. ———. "The Impact of Campus Environments on Student Unrest." Twenty-Fourth National Conference on Higher Education, Chicago, March 3, 1969.

79. ———. "Normal State—A Composite Vignette on the Activities Index and the College Characteristics Index." September 1970. 39 pp. (Mimeo.) The first of nineteen vignettes of the campuses in the Nineteen Campus Study.

*80. ———. *People in Context.* New York: John Wiley & Sons, 1970. Sections on Campus Governance Program Campuses.

81. ———. "The Way the Wind Blows." Twenty-Fifth National Conference on Higher Education, AAHE, March 1970.

The files of the Campus Governance Program also contain a number of unpublished working papers which provide the data for certain of the presentations and publications listed above.

---

* Work using Campus Governance Program data, financial support, or stimulus, but developed primarily under other auspices.

Appendix B.
Acknowledgments

RESPONDENTS

Most of those who have contributed heavily to the Campus Governance Program must go unnamed. They are the administrators, faculty, students, and other staff of almost six hundred campuses which have supplied data on questionnaires or taken part in hundreds of hours of interviews. To protect the anonymity of the campuses, as promised at the outset of the study, we must also omit the names of the leading contributors to the study. Each campus provided a liaison administrator. In the Nineteen Campus Study, extensive help was also provided in administering the Pre-Interview Questionnaire and in arranging for the campus visits of interviewers. The home campuses of the principal researchers have also made extensive contributions in counsel and general support to the staff. Notable in this respect have been Antioch College and Syracuse University.

PLANNING COMMITTEE

The Campus Governance Program was launched in 1966. In the first three years of the Program, the staff had substantial help from the Planning Committee, which discussed, influenced, and gave encouragement to the initial choice of substudies and helped to formulate plans.

The Committee consisted of:

Kenneth Boulding, Center for the Study of Conflict Resolution, University of Michigan

Burton Clark, Professor of Psychology, Yale University

Kenneth B. Clark, Professor of Psychology, City College of New York

John Corson, Brookings Institution

Joseph P. Cosand, President, Junior College District of St. Louis

Merrimon Cuninggim, Executive Director, Danforth Foundation

Ruth Eckert, Professor of Higher Education, University of Minnesota

Samuel B. Gould, President, State University of New York

Robert J. Henle, Vice-President for Academic Administration, St. Louis University

Louis Joughin, American Association of University Professors

Patricia Jean Manion, President, Loretto Heights College

Lewis B. Mayhew, Professor of Education, Stanford University

James Nixon, San Francisco State College

G. Kerry Smith, Chief Executive Officer, AAHE

Sharvy Umbeck, President, Knox College

Stephen Wright, President, AAHE Executive Committee; United Negro College Fund

STAFF

Director:

Morris Keeton, Academic Vice-President, Antioch College

Associate Directors:

Stephen B. Plumer, Assistant Professor of Higher Education and Social Work, Syracuse University; later Associate Professor of Higher Education, Antioch College; later Dean of the Washington-Baltimore Campus, Antioch College

Harold L. Hodgkinson, Dean, Bard College; later Research Associate, Center for Research and Development in Higher Education, University of California at Berkeley

Lawrence Dennis, Associate Executive Secretary, AAHE

SUBSTUDIES

The principal contributors for the three major substudies of the Program are listed here with an indication of their respective roles. Titles are those held at the time of service in the Program.

Task Force on Faculty Representation and Academic Negotiations

Chairman:

Arnold R. Weber, Professor of Industrial Relations, University of Chicago

Members:

Henry H. Bagish, Associate Professor of Sociology and Anthropology, Santa Barbara City College

John F. Burton, Jr., Staff Director of the Task Force, Associate Professor of Industrial Relations and Public Policy, University of Chicago

C. Addison Hickman, Vandeveer Professor of Economics, Southern Illinois University

John C. Livingston, Professor of Government, Sacramento State College

Walter E. Oberer, Professor of Law and Industrial and Labor Relations, Cornell University

Charles M. Rehmus, Professor of Political Science, and Co-Director, Institute of Labor and Industrial Relations, University of Michigan

Frederick R. Livingston, Counsel

Donald H. Wollett, Counsel

The College Trustee Study

Director:

Morton Rauh, Vice-President for Finance, Antioch College

Staff:

Rodney Hartnett, Educational Testing Service

The Nineteen Campus Study

Co-Directors:

Stephen B. Plumer, Assistant Professor of High Education and Social Work, Syracuse University; later Associate Professor of Higher Education, Antioch College; later Dean of the Washington-Baltimore Campus, Antioch College

Harold L. Hodgkinson, Dean, Bard College; later Research Associate, Center for Research and Development in Higher Education, University of California at Berkeley

Research Staff:

Ruth Churchill, College Examiner and Professor of Psychology and Education, Antioch College

George G. Stern, Professor of Psychology, Syracuse University

Michael Metty, Graduate Student at Syracuse University; later Assistant Professor of Education, Antioch College at Columbia, Maryland; later Director of the Center for Social Research and Action, Washington-Baltimore Campus of Antioch College

Suzanne Imes, Research Associate, Antioch College

Ralph Gabrielli, Research Assistant, Syracuse University

Nancy Timmins, Research Assistant, Antioch College

Campus Interviewers:

Staff:

Stephen B. Plumer, Harold G. Hodgkinson, Ruth Churchill, Michael
Metty, Suzanne Imes, Ralph Gabrielli (as listed above)

Faculty and Administrators:

David Underwood, James Dickinson, David Hauser, George Morgan,
Joseph LaBelle, Butler Waugh, W. B. Alexander, Richard Meisler,
Kenneth Freeman, Cathy Bean, Roy Heath, James Findlay, Gates
Agnew, Howard Greenlee, Marvin Knudsen, Philip Rever, James Samp-
son, William Kelly, William Heid, Mary Brigid Niland, Peter Hirsch,
Paul Elsner, Albert Meyer, Robert Kleck, Douglas Palmer, Herbert
Reinelt, Conrad Hilberry, Elden Jacobson, Mary Metz, James Watten-
burger, Anne Murphy, William Arnold, Jack Rossman, Paul Jensen,
William Rogers, C. F. Sleeper, Joseph Bentley, Edward Long

Students:

Ronald Bailey, Rozanne Cole, Charles Beall, Prudence Puff, John
Knox, Martha Lothrop, Edward Rogalski, John Peterson, Carol Smith,
Deborah Clague, Francesca Freedman, Michael Ahmer, William Skocpol,
Theda Skocpol, Roger Byrd, Steven Presser, Frank Stech, Janelle
Gobby, Karl Jost, John Fry, Robert Tanner, William Bergeman, Charles
Derden, John Sahn, Marjorie Witty, Peter Paden, Christina Smith

Critics (consulted on draft manuscript of
Shared Authority on Campus) :

Ralph Brown, Yale University School of Law
C. Addison Hickman, Southern Illinois University
Stanley Ikenberry, Pennsylvania State University
Judson Jerome, Antioch College
John C. Livingston, Sacramento State College
Lewis B. Mayhew, Stanford University
Joyce Varney, Antioch College

Consultants:

Allen Barton, Columbia University
Joseph C. Bentley, Clark University
Abram Bernstein, Syracuse University
Frederick deW. Bolman, Esso Education Foundation
Joseph Katz, Stanford University
Frank Lutz, New York University
Mark Smith, Denison University

Secretaries:

Inge Hyder, Antioch College, Washington-Baltimore Campus
Gwynn James, Antioch College, Washington-Baltimore Campus
Gerda Oldham, Antioch College, Yellow Springs Campus
Frances Pridgen, Antioch College, Washington-Baltimore Campus
Madaline Robison, Antioch College, Washington-Baltimore Campus

AAHE EXECUTIVE AND BOARD

I wish also to acknowledge the strong support of G. Kerry Smith, Chief Executive Officer of the American Association for Higher Education, who had the principal role in obtaining initial support for the Program and in providing the Association's supporting services. The Executive Committee (later Board of Directors) of the Association has provided valuable counsel at the same time that it has scrupulously treated the Program staff as a group entitled to the freedoms typical of the best of faculty personnel practices. The Program began under the presidency of Stephen Wright and has continued through the terms of Lewis B. Mayhew, Addison Hickman, Robert Keller, and Paul Dressel.

Appendix C.
Scales, Sets, and
Categories on the
Pre-Interview
Questionnaire†

Responses from the total group of 3,278 respondents—students, faculty, department chairmen, and administrators from all types of institutions (public and private junior colleges, colleges, and universities)—constituting the largest and broadest study population available, were employed in factoring the Pre-Interview Questionnaire. A principal components analysis of interrelationships among the 120 items led to the extraction of twenty-nine first-order factors with eigenvalues above unity, accounting for 69 percent of the common variance.

Twenty-nine scales were constructed by adding together, one point for each, the responses to all items with loadings of 0.30 or above (equamax rotation) on any factor. All but one of the 120 items met this criterion; the exception—procedures for registration—had six loadings above 0.20, reflecting a diffuse contribution to a number of factors but a primary contribution to no one of them.

The twenty-nine scales were then intercorrelated and refactored, yielding six second-order factors that accounted for 60 percent of the common variance among the scales. The loadings of the scales on these six factors are given in Exhibit 16.

The structure reflected in these six was brought out by scoring them as before and refactoring for a third time. A cut-off of 0.38 was employed, representing the lowest value to include all first-order scales at least once, Scale 21 (student government) being the one in question.

---

† This appendix was prepared by George Stern.

164

Exhibit 16

Second-Order PIQ Factor Loadings

Second-order factors*

		1	2	3	4	5	6	h²
1.	Research resources	.62	.03	.37	.13	—.01	.36	.66
2.	Office services	.74	.00	.04	.22	—.04	.28	.68
3.	Space and resources for student activities	.09	.17	.70	.20	.18	.00	.60
4.	Office space	.87	.02	.15	.07	.10	.11	.81
5.	Regulation of student social behavior	.00	.86	.05	.01	.05	.08	.74
6.	Teaching	—.02	.19	.12	.15	.73	.31	.70
7.	Student identification with the college	—.19	.19	.54	.13	.29	.39	.62
8.	Resources for the arts	.19	.16	.51	.06	.01	.27	.40
9.	Class load and size	.35	.04	.01	.28	.54	.22	.54
10.	Decision-making affecting curriculum	.00	.21	.16	.53	.41	.10	.53
11.	Research and publications	.30	.05	.13	.16	.13	.72	.67
12.	Academic requirements	—.01	.15	.16	.22	.69	.00	.57
13.	Intra-faculty relationships	.42	.06	.00	.23	.03	.64	.65
14.	Faculty-staff relationships	.06	.11	.12	.16	.26	.67	.58
15.	Counseling and advising	.11	.15	.13	.05	.60	.10	.42
16.	Regulation of political behavior	.05	.64	.14	.31	.19	.10	.58
17.	Decision-making affecting faculty	.30	.05	.00	.79	.13	.27	.81
18.	Student and faculty quality	—.01	.14	.14	.39	.15	.48	.45
19.	Library book store and study space	.24	.08	.42	.17	.12	.05	.28
20.	Student dignity	.11	.19	.05	.19	.55	.37	.52
21.	Student government	.01	.28	.27	.26	.38	.04	.37
22.	Parking, transportation and dormitories	.47	.38	.23	.00	.31	—.05	.52
23.	Athletic facilities	.05	.05	.84	.08	.06	.07	.73
24.	Administrative responsiveness to faculty and students	.14	.18	.11	.79	.10	.25	.76
25.	Teaching equipment	.68	.01	.17	.20	.15	.19	.59
26.	Language and science laboratories	.51	.06	.45	.02	.14	.01	.48
27.	Financial support for educ. progress	.69	.04	—.01	.17	.07	.46	.72
28.	Decision-making affecting student life	—.04	.90	.08	.14	.13	.06	.86
29.	Trust	.05	.22	.29	.66	.18	.12	.62
	Σ c²	8.86	3.08	1.80	1.42	1.23	1.07	

* Underlined correlations are those which contribute to the definition of the factor.

Exhibit 17 gives the intercorrelations among the six second-order factors, rearranged now on the basis of their third-order loadings. Two third-order factors were extracted, the first containing 59 percent of the common variance and the second accounting for only 14 percent more. This matrix is in fact highly saturated with some general factor, and it is apparent that we are converging toward it. In effect, these dimensions represent the ills that institutions are heir to; if a school is beset by a number of them in any of the six areas, there is a good chance that it will have problems in the others as well.

Nevertheless, Exhibit 17 is suggestive of a rather interesting state of affairs. Third-order dimensions I and II are most clearly distinguishable from one another by whatever distinguishes second-order factors 1 and 2 from one another, these being the only pair with orthogonal third-order loadings. Factor 1 is based on eight scales dealing largely with the physical resources of the college; factor 2 with student autonomy and academic freedom. To the extent that there is any independence among these factors it is to be found here. A school's problems with its plant and facilities are not likely to be associated with problems of decision making in the areas of social and political behavior.

The pattern among the remaining four factors lends further support to the interpretation of the third-order dimensions as representing institutional resources, on the one hand, and aspects of the interpersonal interactions experience, on the other. There is a broad correspondence between these problem-area dimensions and those aspects of the institutional environment measured by the College Characteristics Index. The structure is summarized in Exhibit 18.

Exhibit 17

Second-Order Matrix and Third-Order Factors, (Pre-Interview Questionnaire)

Second-order intercorrelations							Third-order factors		Second-order factors
							Institutional resources	Inter-personal processes	
1	6	3	4	5	2	h^2	I	II	
—	.74	.47	.47	.40	.31	.82	.90	.12	Physical and financial resources
	—	.56	.65	.58	.36	.74	.86	.33	Faculty and students as resources
		—	.48	.52	.42	.55	.54	.51	Social, esthetic and intellectual resources
			—	.71	.44	.69	.53	.64	Decision-making: academic affairs
				—	.51	.74	.39	.76	The educational milieu
					—	.86	.06	.86	Decision-making: social and political behavior
						Σc^2	3.57	.83	

Exhibit 18

The Factor Composition of the Pre-Interview Questionnaire

Category I—Institutional resources

Factor 1—Physical and financial resources .90

Scales: 4—Office space .87
2—Office services .74
27—Financial support
for educ. progress .69
25—Teaching equipment .68
1—Research resources .62

26—Language and
science laboratories .51
22—Parking, transportation
and dormitories .47
13—Intra-faculty
relationships .42

Factor 6—Faculty and students as resources .86

Scales: 11—Research and
publications .72
14—Faculty-staff relationships .67
13—Intra-faculty relationships .64
18—Student and faculty quality .48

27—Financial support
for educ. progress .46
7—Student identification with
the college .39

Factor 3—Social, esthetic and intellectual resources .54

Scales: 23—Athletic facilities .84
3—Space and resources for
student activities .70
7—Student identification with
the college .54

8—Resources for the arts .51
19—Library, bookstore and
study space .42

Category II—Interpersonal processes

Factor 2—Decision making: Social and political behavior .86

Scales: 28—Decision making affecting
student life .90
5—Regulation of student
social behavior .86

16—Regulation of political
behavior .64
22—Parking, transportation
and dormitories .38

Factor 5—The educational milieu .76

Scales: 6—Teaching .73
12—Academic requirements .69
15—Counseling and advising .60
20—Student dignity .55

9—Class load and size .54
10—Decision making affecting
curriculum .41
21—Student government .38

Factor 4—Decision making: Academic affairs .64

Scales: 17—Decision making
affecting faculty .79
24—Administrative responsiveness
to faculty and students .79
29—Trust .66

10—Decision making affecting
curriculum .53
19—Library, bookstore and
study space .39